Family Literacy

There, perched on a cot I pretended to read. My eyes followed the black signs without skipping a single one and I told myself a story aloud. (Sartre, 1964, p. 48)

*Reproduced courtesy of
the Bergen County Record,
New Jersey*

Cover illustration by Benjamin Taylor

Family Literacy

Young Children Learning to Read and Write

Denny Taylor

Foreword by
Dorothy S. Strickland

Heinemann Educational Books
Exeter, New Hampshire

Heinemann Educational Books Inc.
4 Front Street, Exeter, New Hampshire 03833

LONDON   EDINBURGH   MELBOURNE   AUCKLAND
HONG KONG   SINGAPORE   KUALA LUMPUR
NEW DELHI   IBADAN   NAIROBI   JOHANNESBURG
KINGSTON   PORT OF SPAIN

Library of Congress Cataloging in Publication Data

Taylor, Denny, 1947–
    Family literacy.

    Bibliography: p.
    Includes index.
    1. Literacy.   2. Reading.   3. English language—
Composition and exercises.   4. Family—Books and reading.
I. Title.
LC149.T37   1983   302.2   82-21166
ISBN 0-435-08204-3

Printed in the United States of America

To
my family
David, Louise, and Benjamin.
I love you.

Contents

List of Illustrations

Names and ages
of family members in the study

The Families		Date Entered Study
Lindell	Laura and Barry Sarah and Beth (twins), age 11 Sandy, age 6	September 1977
Dawson	Jessie and Dan Sissie, age 17 Hannah, age 13 Ellie, age 7	November 1977
Farley	Karen and Lee Kathy, age 6 Debbie, age 3 Nan, age 6 months	May 1978
Simms	Nina and Azar Carol, age 6 Andrew, age 3	August 1978
Langdon	Jill and Leo Ken, age 6 Steven, age 3	December 1978
King	Donna and Joe Bonnie, age 7 James, age 2	January 1979

The ages of the children are given at the time they entered the study.

Foreword

Both from a utilitarian and aesthetic standpoint, language is the most marvelous of human possessions. It allows us to share our thoughts, needs, experiences, and feelings. It serves us in a personal way as we internalize new ideas and express our thoughts to others. It serves us in a social manner as it links individuals to society through a shared set of symbols and experiences. Language is the primary means through which cultures are both transmitted and transformed. Today, the importance of effective communication in human society is so pervasive that it influences every aspect of our lives.

Because language is closely linked to the process and product of thought, it serves to mediate virtually all learning. For this reason, the importance of the development of language and literacy in children is considered the first and most fundamental responsibility of the school. It is not surprising that over the years language and literacy have been the subject of more research than any other aspect of education. In recent years, educators from an increasingly expanding number of disciplines have been studying literacy development and its influence on the total growth of the child. Anthropologists, sociologists, philosophers, and psychologists are all apt to consider the functions of language and literacy as they affect human development.

Currently, we are experiencing a period of exciting and highly productive research in the development of child language and literacy. This research has moved beyond the traditional concern for the acquisition of form, structures, and skills to focus attention on the context of learning. The new research draws upon psycholinguistics, sociolinguistics, anthropology, child development, cognitive psychology, and educational research for its theories and methodologies. It focuses on how people behave and learn in natural settings as a means to inform educational theory and practice. An underlying assumption of the new research is that just as language cannot be separated from the development of thinking, neither can it be separated from the context in which it is learned. The observation and analysis of children's literacy development in natural settings hold exciting promise for the extension of our knowledge of how children become effective readers and writers and of the contextual factors that may support or constrain that development.

Family Literacy is consistent with the new approach to studying how people develop language competence. Focusing on family interaction, Taylor offers an abundance of evidence about how the family serves to support the development of literacy in children. An extraordinarily effective communicator herself, Taylor writes with such skill and sensitivity that the effect is a scholarly work that engages the reader much as a good novel would. As the absorbing stories of the six children and their families unfolds chapter by chapter, one begins to grasp the complexity of the human interaction described and to appreciate the many ways it contributes to the development of literacy.

Family Literacy is an important contribution to the state of our knowledge about literacy development in children. It comes at a time when academic programs and materials are often at odds with what research tells us about how children become literate. It is a book for teachers, parents, researchers and all those who are concerned with providing supportive contexts for children's learning. It is a book that celebrates families, children, literacy, and all those who take pride in helping children become readers and writers.

Dorothy S. Strickland
Teachers College
Columbia University
New York

Preface

One cannot take linguistic form, a given code, or even speech itself, as a limiting frame of reference. One must take as context a community, or network of persons, investigating its communicative activities as a whole, so that any use of channel and code takes its place as part of the resources upon which the members draw. (Hymes, 1974, p. 4)

From T-shirts to bubble gum wrappers, children live in a world fashioned in print. Few can escape the abundance of words that fill their homes, and yet we know very little about that world or its effect on learning to read and write in schools.

My interest in the family and literacy began in 1968 when I started teaching in the East End of London. When you have 41 five-, six-, and seven-year-old children and only 20 "Janet and John" books, you look for help. My school days began early and ended late as I made books and prepared materials, but my greatest resource was the children's families. Without them, I would not have made it through the first year. Each night after school, I talked with parents about the activities of the day and gave them their children's reading books so they could read together at home. As we talked and I came to know these families, I realized that they knew more than I of the children and their learning. Their lives hovered beyond my reach, and the wealth of local understandings were never quite within my grasp.

In 1974, I came to the States to study reading. For the next three years, I was steeped in the clinical applications of this psycholinguistic process. It was an intellectually stimulating time when researchers in reading were moving away from curriculum-based research to theory-based research focusing upon the process of reading. But I became uncomfortably conscious that we were creating learning environments for children where reading and writing were presented as decontextualized language skills largely unconnected to reading and writing in everyday life. My East End families came back to me, but their lives seemed more elusive than ever. The memory of these families provided me with the incentive to look for new ways of approaching literacy research. As Medawar argues in his advice to a young scientist, "The greatest incentive to learning a new skill or supporting discipline is the urgent need to use it" (1979, p. 40).

Thus, I found myself in the Department of Family and Community Education at Teachers College, Columbia University, with Professor Herve Varenne, a French anthropologist, as my mentor. My study of family literacy began at that time and culminated in my doctoral dissertation. My task was to develop systematic ways of looking at reading and writing as activities that have consequences in and are affected by family life. Six families participated in the research, and each one had a child who was considered by his/her parents to be successfully learning to read and write at the time the family entered into the study.

When the study began in 1977, I hoped to match the writing to the fieldwork, as I wanted to establish reciprocity between these two equally important aspects of the research process. The writing began on the first day of the study, and since that time the research and writing processes have continued in tandem. As the research evolved and the writing proceeded, I was continuously aware that I must produce a "scholarly" work for my doctoral committee as well as a text that I could share with the participating families. Since then, the text has been reorganized, the footnotes and appendices have been removed, and some sections have been rewritten.

It is now late 1982, and the research which began in 1977 as a solitary endeavor has become a collaborative venture. I have been joined by Catherine Dorsey-Gaines, and together we are working with families who are living below the poverty level in a decaying urban neighborhood. It is an area of abandoned buildings and vacant lots, but despite overwhelming problems children are learning to read and write, and we are finding homes filled with print. Over the next three years, we will watch the progress of these children as we try to find out more of how their families' personal biographies and educative styles shape their literate experiences.

I hope the present book will encourage others to join us in this venture so we can learn more of the many ways children growing up in a variety of settings initiate, absorb, and synthesize the cultural complexities of learning to read and write.

Acknowledgments

I wish to convey my very sincere thanks to the many people whose help and support made the research project possible.

I owe a special debt of gratitude to Professor Herve Varenne who sponsored the study. He is a true mentor and friend. My sincere thanks also go to Professor Hope Jensen Leichter for her constant encouragement throughout the three years of the project; and to Professor Anne McKillop and Professor Dorothy Strickland, members of my doctoral committee, for their support and interest in the project.

I also want to express the very deep sense of gratitude that I feel for the families who shared their lives with me. Their support of the project merits a special thank you.

D. T.

1

The Families

The family is an arena in which virtually the entire range of human experience can take place. (Leichter, 1974, p. 1)

Schneider (1968) states, "The best that can be said for an anthropologist is that he has a good bunch of informants" (p. 8). I would agree with Schneider and would add that there is more than a degree of serendipity in finding families to study. However, logical steps can be taken. My guiding factor was that each of the families had one child who was considered by the parents to be successfully learning to read and write. The research began in September 1977 with the study of a single family, and gradually, as new questions arose, more families were invited to participate, until January 1979 when six families were actively involved in the study. As the research proceeded and new families were sought, theoretical sampling procedures were employed (Glaser and Strauss, 1973) in which the perspective presented by Beattie (1964) became an important consideration. Beattie stresses that it is more useful to make comparisons between institutions (in this instance, the family) that have similar backgrounds and contexts. He emphasizes that there may be great differences in the social significance of that which is described, adding that, "To compare things implies that in at least some respect they are different as well as that they are similar, and differences are only meaningful against comparable backgrounds" (p. 48). Rather than pursue any notion of sociological representation, for this study I selected families that, although differing with respect to education and religious affiliation, might generally be described as white middle class, living in suburban towns within a fifty-mile radius of New York City. Thus the notion of comparability was established, and variations could be explored.

I met the six families participating in the study at different times and in different places, but in each case I was the newcomer. I met the Lindells* in 1974, just after my arrival in the United States. Laura

* The names of the individuals participating in the study have been changed to protect their anonymity.

and her three children stopped by on a snowy April day to welcome me to the neighborhood; we have been friends ever since. In 1977, we moved again—this time to the same neighborhood as the Dawsons and Farleys. While living there I met the Simms, Langdon, and King families. We have moved again, but the families are still close enough for me to visit.

There were a number of reasons for my inviting the Lindells to participate in the study. At the time the project began, Sandy, their youngest child, had just entered first grade, and Laura often commented on how well she was learning to read. In addition, I knew many of the families with whom the Lindells socialized and the children with whom Sandy and her older twin sisters, Sarah and Beth, played. It was therefore possible for me to see them as part of a larger social group as well as a family unit. Of equal importance was the fact that I had established access to the family without intrusion (Taylor, 1981). As a neophyte to fieldwork, I wanted to work with a family that was easy in my company, that would put up with my blunders and laugh at my eccentricities. The Lindells fit the bill; they met the research criteria and we were friends.

The Lindells live by a lake in a fading rural town which was once a popular summertime residence for New Yorkers. Over the years the builders have made their mark, and although there are still two horse farms and some cornfields, the impression is one of merging developments as the town has become a part of the urban sprawl. Even the lake has been affected by the change; it is too polluted for swimming and the bottom is muddied with silt.

The Lindells' heritage is one of affluence and poverty. Laura comes from a wealthy New England family, and her grandmother was a celebrated writer of gothic novels. Barry comes from a working-class family; he grew up in a deteriorating inner-city neighborhood, and his father died of alcoholism. Through hard work and with the aid of scholarships, Barry was accepted at an Ivy League university where he studied for a doctorate in marine biology. Here he met Laura who was working in the university's zoological museum. After Barry completed his doctorate, the couple married and lived in several locations before they settled into their lakeside home, which is close to the university where Barry is a professor.

In November 1977, I was ready to add a second family to the study. I wanted a family that fulfilled the research criteria, but I wished to vary the educational level of the parents. I invited the Dawsons to participate in the study. I had spoken with Jessie on several occasions while watching my children play in the street, and she told me of how well Ellie, her youngest daughter, was doing in school.

The Dawson family lives in a quietly prosperous town which has the distinct advantage of having a main street that is not a major throughway. They have lived in the town for twelve years, but Jessie and her husband, Dan, often talk of moving north to a more rural setting. Their house is part of a development built in the fifties, and the family describes it as being rather ugly. However ugly the house is on the outside, it is invitingly pretty on the inside.

Jessie Dawson's parents were divorced, and as a child she lived with her mother. When Jessie finished high school she took a business course and got a job as a secretary with an engineering company. She met Dan who was also employed by the company, and they were married when she was twenty-one. Dan's parents were also divorced. His younger brother and sister lived with his mother, while he lived with various members of his family. At different times he stayed with his father, his grandfather, and his aunts, and for a while when he was fifteen he lived on his own working as a fire fighter for a forestry commission and traveling with a circus. During his teenage years, Dan became very interested in engineering and served an apprenticeship in mechanical engineering. Today Dan is an entrepreneur with a patented process for decreasing pollutants in automobile emissions. When the study began, Jessie was dividing her time between her secretarial commitments and her volunteer work in the library of Ellie's school where she read stories to children. These occasions were a great success, and Jessie was offered a part-time position as an aide working with the children in the library. Today Jessie works full time at the school, helping the children select books and reading stories to first, second, and third graders. She enjoys working with the children and is presently considering going back to school to gain a BA. There are three children in the Dawson family. In November 1977, Sissie was seventeen, Hannah was thirteen, and Ellie was seven. Ellie seldom played outside at that time, because like her father, she was acutely asthmatic. But over the past two years she seems to have built up some tolerance to the irritants that plagued her, and she can now play for many hours outside with her friends.

Six months later I considered adding a third family. In addition to the information I was collecting about Sandy Lindell and Ellie Dawson learning to read and write, I was accumulating many retrospective accounts of their older siblings' early literate experiences. These recollections raised many questions that I wanted to explore with families who had preschool children. The Farleys were such a family. Debbie Farley was three years and five months, and Nan Farley was just six months of age in May 1978 when the family entered the study; Kathy Farley, concluding her kindergarten year, was beginning to read. Karen had commented to me that Kathy was already in a reading group at school, and that she was finding it easy to learn to read. In addition, the Dawsons and the Farleys were friends. Ellie Dawson and Kathy Farley often played together, and Sissie and Hannah Dawson often baby-sat for Karen and Lee Farley. Once again, I was able to place the families in a larger social context.

Karen Farley is an only child, and her mother was nearing forty when she was born. Karen's was a quiet childhood. Her mother speaks of her as a private person who was content to spend much of her time on her own; she still enjoys her own company. In the afternoons while her children sleep she works on sewing projects or posters for the PTA, protecting her time with a sign which reads NAPPING taped to the front door. Karen studied art at a college she describes as a small school in a quiet town. At college she met Lee who was a political science major. They were married the year of their graduation and made their home in New York City. Lee spent his childhood in a town very close to the one where the family is now living. He was one of three boys, and his mother remembers them as very active. Lee himself has said that they "bounced all over the place" and often got into trouble with the neighbors. Lee speaks of himself as an average student, emphasizing that he was never "a student kind of person." When he finished college, Lee wanted to enter banking but was told that the most he could expect was a position in personnel. Lee began to study; today he is a banking executive with a graduate degree in bank management.

In the summer of 1978, I was particularly interested in finding families with young sons to participate in the study. Working with the Lindells, Dawsons, and Farleys had already stimulated my interest in family story-reading occasions, and I was spending much of my time talking with storytellers and actively participating in the story hours at a library in a nearby town. I met Nina Simms and Jill Langdon at a story hour. They were attending a series of mother-child story sessions with their young sons, Andrew and Steven, who were then three years of age. I attended the story hours for a month before talking with Nina and Jill about my research interest in young children learning to read and write. Nina told me that her daughter Carol had learned to read in kindergarten, while Jill spoke of her older son Ken who was about to enter first grade. Ken was not reading and Jill voiced her concern about his progress.

In August 1978, Nina Simms said her family would be pleased to take part in my research. The Simms family lives in a multiracial neighborhood in a suburban town. They own a small fifty-year-old colonial house which is filled with family living. Nina is the first to admit that she hates housework, and Azar, her husband, speaks of the house being uncomfortably small. However, their home is chaotically friendly and easy to visit.

Nina grew up in the Bronx with her mother, father, and two young brothers. Her maternal grandmother lived in the opposite apartment with her aunt and uncle, and her paternal grandmother lived upstairs. When Nina was twelve years old her mother died, and she and her brothers went to live in a foster home. Two years later her father remarried, and the boys lived with him while Nina lived with her aunt's family. When Nina finished high school, she got a job as a bookkeeper, eventually becoming the supervisor of the credit card department of a large oil company. In 1960, she went on a blind date and met Azar. They were married two and a half years later. Azar was working for an import and export business when he met Nina. He had grown up in Afghanistan and had come to the United States after the Second World War to join his uncle in the family import and export business. In 1956, Afghanistan nationalized such companies, and Azar's uncle returned home. Azar decided to stay and took a position in a similar company. Today he is employed by another such firm and works in the traffic department organizing the transportation of goods.

I waited until December before asking the Langdon family to participate in the study. By that time Ken Langdon, who was in first grade, was well on the way to becoming a reader, and his parents, Jill and Leo, talked of how pleased they were with his progress. The Langdon family's friendship with the Simms family was an added advantage. Jill Langdon and Nina Simms shared many activities, while Ken Langdon and his younger brother Steven often played with Carol Simms and her younger brother Andrew.

The Langdon family lives in an old colonial house on a street quite close to the home of the Simms family. Jill Langdon was born in Minnesota. When Jill finished high school she attended business courses and did office work until she was old enough to become a stewardess for a major airline. Her job brought her to New York where she met Leo. They were married two years later and made their home in New York City. Leo is a native New Yorker. At the time he met Jill he was working during the day and going to school at night to get his undergraduate degree. Leo has two brothers and a sister, and he describes his family as a middle-class Catholic family in which the children were oriented toward religion. He attended parochial schools and says he has "very bad feelings" about the nuns who taught him during his elementary years. His memories are of their stringent discipline. Leo spent his draft years in Germany, and after he returned he decided to study for a degree. Today he is the manager of a department that processes legal claims for a large engineering company.

In January 1979, I invited the final family to participate in the study. I wanted to add a family who knew one of the other families. Donna King lives just a few blocks from Karen Farley, and I had met her on several occasions when visiting Karen. Donna's daughter Bonnie was in first grade with Kathy Farley, and the two mothers often talked about their daughters. Donna spoke of how Bonnie was making good progress in school and of her enjoying learning to read. Since Bonnie had a preschool brother and I already had access to members of their social network, they fitted easily into the research.

Donna grew up on the West Coast surrounded by grandparents, aunts, and uncles with whom she stayed from time to time. While she was working on a master's degree in psychology she met Joe who was a doctoral candidate at the same university. Joe is also from the West Coast. Of his childhood, he speaks of his father, an immigrant from Europe, who worked until 9:00 or 10:00 at night and then came home to fall asleep in the chair. Joe emphasizes that he was not interested in school and that all his free time was devoted to sports. He says that he played baseball and football in the street with his friends from the time he got home from school until seven or eight at night. Once Donna and Joe had completed their degrees, they moved to the East Coast where Donna began studying for a doctorate and Joe embarked on post-doctoral research. Since that time, Joe has become an administrator, and Donna has worked off and on as a counselor.

These then are the six families who helped me. The Lindells, the Dawsons, the Farleys, the Simmses, the Langdons, and the Kings, all welcomed me into their homes and supported my efforts as I tried to gain a better understanding of what I have come to refer to as family literacy.

2

Family Literacy: Conservation and Change in the Transmission of Literacy Styles and Values

There are two principles inherent in the very nature of things, recurring in some particular embodiments whatever field we explore—the spirit of change, and the spirit of conservation. There can be nothing real without both. Mere change without conservation is a passage from nothing to nothing. Its final integration yields mere transient non-entity. Mere conservation without change cannot conserve. For after all, there is a flux of circumstance and the freshness of being evaporates under mere repetition. (Whitehead, 1925, p. 201)

Early in the study, I was impressed by the way the parents moved easily between the past and present as they talked about their own experiences of learning to read and write and the experiences of their children. In each family, some rituals and routines of written language usage appear to conserve family traditions of literacy, while others appear to change the patterns of the past. The patterns of family literacy are constantly evolving to accomodate the everyday experiences of both parents and children; the introduction of a younger sibling can lead to the systematic restructuring of the routine. In analyzing the data it has become increasingly evident that the most significant "mode" of transmitting literacy styles and values occurs indirectly, at the very margins of awareness (Leichter, 1974) through the continuously diffuse use of written language in the ongoing life of the family. The direct transmission of literacy styles and values through specific learning encounters occurs less frequently, and such didactic occasions are spasmodic, usually occurring in response to some school-related situation.

MEMORIES OF THE PAST
AND INTERPRETATIONS OF THE PRESENT

Parents' Memories
Reminiscing, Laura Lindell spoke of "the long trek" to Maine her family had made when she was two years of age, and she spoke of the

funny things that had happened. She explained, "There was an out house and I had my potty chair and I used it one day without the pot and was amazed!" It would seem that such memories remain clear as the years pass. Jessie Dawson spoke of the flowered wallpaper in her bedroom, and Lee Farley of the swing that had seemed to go "two miles high." Dan Dawson spoke of planting radishes with his father, and Nina Simms of her predilection for getting lost. She recounted gleefully:

> There was a snowstorm and I was gone again as usual. Finally my father goes to the police station and there I am on the captain's desk eating lollipops and ice cream and all bundled up. The policeman says to me, "Is this your father?" And I say "No!" (Laughs.) So my father was ready to choke me and he had to show all kinds of identification that he was my father and then carry me home in the snow.

Memories of "literate things" were much slower to surface. All of the parents had some memories of print being a part of family life and of their parents' involvement with print (such as reading the newspapers), but few could remember specific occasions designed to introduce them to written language. Lee Farley said that both his parents had read a lot, and Leo Langdon presented a similar picture, but both men emphasized that they had not been read to by their parents.

Leo Langdon stated that he had no recollection of having any books except when he went to school.

> I don't remember my parents reading to me and I'm not saying they didn't but I have no real recollection. I remember, it's funny when you start thinking about it, I remember my grandparents. My grandmother used to read the comics to me . . . but I remember and the reason I remember is because at times people would say, "Do you remember your grandmother reading comics to you?" or something like that. They would say that to me, and that's probably why I remember.

Similarly, Joe King, who spoke of his parents as immigrants and of his background as "impoverished," said that his mother had read to him: "the sense I have is that my mother used to read to me all the time, but it's a sense I have and I've been told that." Barry Lindell's memories of his early years were difficult to face, and he spoke of trying to suppress as much as he could. He commented, "None of the people in my family were very good readers . . . it wasn't important." Barry said that no one had read to him, adding, "It's absolutely amazing that with the amount of reading I do now that I did virtually none and my parents did very little." Although Barry's impression was that his family did not read, he did speak of his father reading the newspaper "regularly every night." Only Laura Lindell and Jessie Dawson spoke of being read to on a regular basis. Laura listened to her father reading adventure stories to her brothers, while Jessie was read to "just about every day" by her mother as well as by her grandmother and her aunts, who had helped raise her after her parents' divorce. For Dan Dawson, there was little regularity in his early years, but there was a time when he too had been read to by his father and grandfather. Dan spoke of the afternoon when his grandfather returned home with a new book: "He taught me to read, it seemed to me, in one afternoon." For many of the parents, their memories of being read to were locked inside stories of long-forgotten books. Donna King spoke of reading *Peter Rabbit* to her children and realizing the story was familiar to her; Jill Langdon spoke of a book she had found at the library and of the repetitive line "Scat, scat, go away little cat," which she had loved as a child; and Karen Farley spoke of rediscovering *Little House*, which she vaguely remembered her mother reading to her as a small child. For these parents, recollections were triggered by the books they read their children. Listening to stories was deeply embedded in the recesses of the past and much more difficult to retrieve than the memories of observing their parents read. Although Karen Farley had few memories of being read to as a child, she had very clear memories of seeing her father reading engineering books and of enjoying the feeling of the bumpy leather on the spines of the texts.

School Memories

Only Jessie Dawson and Karen Farley had pleasant memories of their first-grade year. Jessie spoke of sitting in a circle with a book in her lap:

> We sat in a circle with the teacher and we had flash cards she would hold up and we would be told what the words were and we would go through an exercise where they were shown to us again and we could call them out as we saw them. Then she would put that away and we would open the book and there would be those words and you could read them. I remember very clearly sitting in that circle.

Karen Farley recalled the excitement of getting a new reader, and she spoke of how happy she was when she was allowed to take a book home, because it seemed like homework. Laura Lindell's memories were very different. When I asked her if she remembered being taught to read in school, she said, "No. I don't remember it because I remember feeling bored by their way of doing it with the traditional Dick and Jane and Sally the little sister and Puff and Spot and all the happy clean faces." Dan Dawson also remembered thinking of it as "kind of dull." Barry Lindell learned to read easily in school, but remembered it as an anxious time. He said that one of the things that bothered him was that so many of the children could not read; he added, "They would falter over little words and I would get very anxious and want to go over and read it for them."

Leo Langdon spoke of his "mixed emotions" about the parochial grammar school he attended and of the harsh discipline which he so clearly remembers. Leo said he had great difficulty learning to read and had been in sixth grade when he finally began to read. However, Leo emphasized that it was not until he was in the army that he became a reader. Stuck in West Germany with time on his hands, he occupied himself reading the paperbacks other men left lying around. Lee Farley spoke of learning to read as probably the worst experience of his entire life, and speaking of some of the ways that reading was taught he said:

> Oh, I can remember those agonies but I don't know when that was, of passing the story around the room deal. "OK, Johnny, you read the first four sentences." (Groans and pretends to read.) "Your turn Lee." And you go (strangled sound) (laughs), you just choke right there. God, I read badly. To this day I have difficulty spelling anything except my name. That was probably the worst experience of my life . . . I think probably that is the most humiliating, embarrassing, and most horrible thing that teachers do to kids. Maybe it was just because I was the one who couldn't do it. "It's your turn to read," and you didn't even know what page they were on. (Laughs.) I was off someplace but even if I knew what page they were on and you read over a word and you botch the word and you didn't know what it was or they make you "sound it out." You didn't even know what it sounded like. Yuk. No (laughs), I don't remember enjoying that ever.

Like Leo, Lee was an adult when he became a reader. Stimulated by his desire for a career in banking, Lee began to read the relevant literature, and today the *Wall Street Journal* is his standard fare.

Throughout the discussions of their childhood experiences, the parents often referred to the experiences of their children, and they found it as difficult to talk about their children's preschool involvement with written language as it was to speak of their own preschool experiences. Occasionally they mentioned their early interest in writing and drawing, and the interest of their children in such activities, but it was only when examples of the children's work were collected for this study that they became aware of the amount of drawing and writing that was taking place on a daily basis.

The only activity which was repeatedly mentioned by the parents was the reading of stories to their children, and in this context the literacy styles and values that they wished to impart to their children were in some ways made "visible." On different occasions, Laura Lindell spoke of her great interest in books, her father's love of literature, and her children's enjoyment of books. She attributed her children's interest to the fact that they had always listened to stories at bedtime, and speaking of their early years she said, "They loved finding out what was between the covers; if they ripped them it didn't matter; they ate them and they teethed on them." Barry also spoke of when the children had been babies, and he emphasized that they had read to them "as soon as their eyes could focus." Based upon the many occasions that Laura and Barry have talked about reading stories, it would seem that Laura is conserving patterns of literate language use while Barry is attempting to change the patterns of his past.

THE JUXTAPOSITIONING OF CHILDHOOD EXPERIENCES

The conservation of literacy styles and values occurs almost automatically, and only when the parent is intent on change is a conscious effort involved. Laura never spoke of reading to her children because her father had read to her, but Barry did speak of not being read to as a child and of how important he felt it was for his children to listen to stories. Similarly, Karen Farley read stories to her children, and the only linkages she made with her own childhood were her comments when she found that a story she was reading to her children was one she had heard as a child, whereas Lee Farley was conscious of wishing to provide alternate experiences for his children. Speaking of his own experiences, he stated,

> Yes, the books were around, yes, we read, but I don't remember anybody sitting down and saying, "Gee, isn't this fun?" as opposed to "You've got to do it!" And it's something, when I work with her (Kathy) I (say), "Hey, let's try this! Won't this be fun!"

As Lee spoke, it was clear that he wanted to change patterns of his past, and as he stated when speaking of Kathy, "Maybe I know that because I hated it so badly I'm going to guarantee her that she doesn't know that I disliked it so much."

Parents Vis-à-Vis One Another

In each of the families, the evolution of literacy transmission is highly dependent on the childhood experiences of the parents and evolves through the interplay of their individual biographies and educative styles. Yet, although each of the parents was aware of the background of his or her partner, they had not specifically discussed with each other the literate experiences that they wanted for their children. Without implying any general statement of harmony, it appeared that the parents had evolved complementary roles without planning explicit strategies. Laura Lindell commented that "it had just happened that way." She said that she had naturally given the children books when they were "at the eating stage," and that she thought Barry had taken his cues from her. Karen Farley said that there were so many other things that they had to deal with on a daily basis that "reading had never been an issue," and she added that if at some time in the future one of the children were to have a problem, she was sure that they would discuss it. Once, Karen was talking about the activities that her children enjoyed in the magazine *Cricket*, and I asked her if she ever helped them with these activities. She replied:

> It's hard, I think it's very hard to find the time. Mainly when they do it is when Lee comes home . . . I do the more practical things, but when he comes home he's fresh for them, and they're so anxious to show him and he even gets a kick out of doing these things.

The Mediation of Past Experiences: An Idiosyncratic Process

In looking at the ways the parents shared literate experiences with their children, it was found that through the interplay of the personal biographies and educative styles of the parents comparable childhood experiences were mediated in different ways. The childhood experiences of Leo Langdon were very similar to those of Lee Farley. Both men had found it difficult to learn to read and had spoken of the social humiliation of the experience, and both men wished to ensure that their children did not suffer similar experiences. However, this is where the similarities end, for the men have evolved very different styles in working with their children. Lee Farley is actively intent upon making it fun for his children to play with print, while Leo Langdon is attempting to ensure that his children are not pressured into learning to read before they are ready. He has bided his time, and it was only when Ken was in first grade and learning to read without any difficulty that he began to participate in his reading and writing activities.

The different approaches that Lee Farley and Leo Langdon evolved in their transmission of literary skills and values illustrate that the mediation of past experiences is an idiosyncratic process which can result in very different experiences for individual children who are nevertheless successful in learning to read.

THE PARENTS' MEDIATION
OF THE LITERATE EXPERIENCES OF THEIR CHILDREN

There are also differences within each family in the ways the parents mediate the literate experiences of individual children. The first born appears to be influenced to a large degree by the experiences of the parents, whereas the second child is greatly affected by the family's interpretations of the experiences of the first born and by the interaction which takes place between the children. The process is both active and reactive, as all family members are influenced by the changing dynamics of family life, triggered by the inclusion of another child within the group.

First Borns

First borns are a mixed blessing. The parents in each of the families had looked forward to parenting; however, the reality of becoming a parent was not always the experience they had anticipated. Laura Lindell, in particular, was not prepared. She had planned for one baby, and with no advance warning she gave birth to two. Laura spoke of the mothering of two babies as a completely overwhelming experience. The experience of Jill Langdon was very similar to that of Laura, and she spoke of when Ken was born as "a very unsettling time." Lee Farley said that he was sure that Karen had not slept for the first month after Kathy's birth, and Karen herself recalled that she was concerned because Kathy was so timid. She said, "I worried and worried about her and I remember bringing it up with the pediatrician." Each family emphasized the amount of time spent caring for the first child. Lee Farley represented the consensus when he said, "I feel you heap more attention on the first one than you'll probably give to anyone else again no matter how hard you try."

Parents spoke of reading to the first-born child from a very early age, and they emphasized the active role that the child had taken in the story-reading occasion. Karen Farley's comments about reading to Kathy illustrate the ways the personal agendas of parent and child come together in the newness of the situation. Karen related,

> Well, she had always been read to and I seemed to spend a great deal of time with her because I was so concerned about being a new mother, doing things with her the whole time. . . . I don't know, so much of it is Kathy. She had that ability to catch on to things quickly, to absorb it, and to play it back.

Donna King also emphasized the active role Bonnie had played during the story-sharing occasions, and she recalled that from a very young age Bonnie would come to her with a book for her to read. However, not all the children were so inclined toward listening to stories. Jessie Dawson remembered that Sissie did not like to sit still for long and although she liked picture books she had a very short attention span, and so Jessie could not read to her as much as she would have liked. From Jessie's comments, it would seem that Sissie was quite active in shaping the literate experiences that she shared with her mother.

Siblings

During the many discussions that focused on the children, the parents spoke of their subsequent children as fitting into the established patterns of family life. Laura Lindell spoke of Sandy learning by "osmosis," and she emphasized that she "just had to adapt." Karen Farley, speaking of Nan, said, "I just think of her as being very calm and of fitting into the group and of going along with it." Jessie Dawson spoke specifically of reading when she said that Ellie had naturally listened to stories; she explained "We had developed a habit of reading when Ellie was born. Sissie was nine and Hannah was six." In such ways, the established patterns were conserved, but also changes were made, some of them quite basic. Caring for two children requires considerable orchestration, and each family mentioned that in the rush of coping, the second child received less parental attention than the first child had. Jill Langdon made this point when she said, "I can remember times when Steven cried and I was going to tend to him and something else would come up, Ken would be running outside, and by the time I'd straightened that out the baby maybe had stopped crying."

Other changes were stimulated by the children themselves. The parents spoke of the differences they perceived, juxtaposing the characteristics of their children as they described the differences. Azar Simms talked of Andrew and Carol in this way. He said he felt that Andrew had an excellent attention span. He laughed and went on to say that Andrew was like a spider, that he would spend hours tying all sorts of objects together—chairs, tables, and so on— until the whole room was tied in knots. Azar then spoke of Carol, and he stated that she did not have such an attention span and that she would often flit from one thing to another.

The parents also made sharp contrasts between their children in literate areas. Joe King shared his observation of Donna reading to Bonnie, and he explained that she sat quietly, intently listening to the stories. Characterizing the experience that Donna and Bonnie had shared, he said, "It's almost a hypnotic effect. . . . You don't even need to listen to the words; it's like a mother talking to a child; it's that kind of rapport." Of James, Joe related that he enjoyed talking about the story more than listening to the printed words, and he added that James let him "know what was happening" in more ways than Bonnie, who had always been content to sit and listen.

In talking of their children, the parents hinted at the difficulties which arose as they tried to balance the conservation of the patterns established by the family with the changes necessitated by the needs of individual children. Nina Simms presented an example at the beginning of the study when she expressed her concern at Andrew's lack of interest in such activities as coloring and painting. Nina said that, although she provided him with the materials as she had done for Carol, Andrew preferred to build and play with trucks. These difficulties are also illustrated by the comments of Lee Farley when he was speaking of Kathy and her younger sister Debbie. In his attempts to ensure that Kathy enjoyed her early experiences of written language, Lee played many games with her, but Debbie was not interested in these games. While conserving his need to provide his children with good experiences of print, Lee was forced to change his strategies. What worked with Kathy was not working with Debbie. Lee commented,

> She's not showing the interest in it and the last thing I feel inspired to do is ram it down her throat kind of routine: "Here. Sit down we'll look at words!" (said crossly). I mean, fine, when we look at words we'll look at words. When the opportunity is there we'll do it but she doesn't want to play the game. For Kathy it was a challenge, it was a game, a new word. Debbie doesn't quite see it that way so OK, we'll try a little different approach. I don't know what.

It would seem that while Lee was conscious of wanting to provide Debbie with the same guarantee that he offered to Kathy, he realized that it must be couched in different terms and with different provisions. Restructuring was necessary. During the year following this conversation, Lee played few games with Debbie, but he continued to read to her on a regular basis. Interestingly, when Debbie was five and in her last year of nursery school she became interested in playing with print at school, and both Lee and Karen supported her in these activities.

On another level, it is not only the difference between children which contributes to the different ways in which the parents worked with their children. This is well illustrated by Donna King's remarks when she listened to an audio recording of a story she had read with James. She said:

> I sure was frustrated with him. I don't know, in a sense I'm not sure whether it's a difference in him or in terms of what I've gotten used to. I have a sense that in general I've gotten used to reading to Bonnie, and reading the story. I'm more impatient about looking at the pictures and talking about the pictures and so forth than I might have been with her when she was at that age or at that stage in terms of looking at pictures and talking about them.

Donna's comments emphasize the ways the parents changed as they engaged in, moved through, and combined educational experiences over time (Leichter, 1973, 1978).

Siblings Vis-à-Vis One Another

In *The Sibling*, Sutton-Smith and Rosenberg (1970) write "siblings make each other different" (p. 2). In each family, the parents spoke of how their children influenced one another. Again, the data suggest that both older and younger siblings are active and reactive in shaping the literate experiences of each other. The parents emphasized the amount of time their children spent together. Jill Langdon spoke of Steven's relationship with Ken, his older brother. Speaking of Steven as a baby, she said, "He had someone else to watch and watching Ken was much more interesting than watching me. He would do things that were much more interesting to a child than the things that I do." Karen Farley made similar comments, while Donna King emphasized that although James had missed having his parents to himself, he enjoyed his interactions with his sister Bonnie, and that he had many experiences which Bonnie as a first born had missed.

Parents spoke of the younger children listening to their older sibling(s) read. Beth and Sarah Lindell both read stories to Sandy, and Sissie and Hannah Dawson read to Ellie. Nina Simms said that when she was busy, she often asked Carol to read to Andrew, and once when Carol was reading stories to me Andrew joined us, listening to the story and echoing his sister's words as she spoke. Kathy Farley reads to Debbie at bedtime. Debbie has often spoken of her sister reading to her, and Karen has spoken of Kathy reading to Nan. Two years ago, Karen spoke of Kathy propping Nan up in her pumpkin seat when she was only six months old so that she could see the pictures as Kathy read her a story. However, the data indicate that although emphasis was given to older siblings reading stories to younger siblings, this did not occur as regularly as the reading of stories by parents. The children read together spasmodically, and these events were influenced by many factors, including whether the older child wanted to read and the younger child wanted to listen and finding time for such an activity in the bustle of daily living.

On another level, the children were interacting with print daily, but the extent of this activity was only hinted at by the parents. Parents occasionally mentioned that individual children liked to draw or write, and they sometimes spoke of them writing with or to friends. But much went by unnoticed, and it was only when examples of the children's work were collected that the extent of their involvement became evident and this part of their lives became available for discussion. However, it should be emphasized that the children are interacting with print on a daily basis and that siblings and friends are mediating each other's literate experiences.

THE FAMILY'S MEDIATION
OF SCHOOL EXPERIENCE OF LEARNING TO READ AND WRITE

For the families taking part in this study, the sum total of their literate experiences comes into play in the mediation of each child's learning to read and write in school. The experiences of the parents, the experiences of brothers and sisters, and the child's own experiences form a filter through which learning at school must pass. In each of the families, the parents were critical of the schools their children attended and of the methods by which they were taught; however, they were also supportive of the schools. I mentioned this interpretation to the parents. During my discussion with Jill Langdon she elaborated on her and her husband's criticisms of the teachers and the teaching methods—while at the same time being supportive of the system. Jill explained that at the beginning of Ken's second-grade year she had been quite concerned because she disliked the teacher. She said that the teacher had a voice "like gravel" which "grated on you," and she added that the teacher did not have a good relationship with the children. Jill then spoke of how Leo had impressed upon her that she should not let Ken know she was upset because it would confuse him. Jill said Leo had emphasized their supporting the school as it was important for Ken to feel that his school learning was important.

The parents also played an active role in school activities. Most of the parents attended school meetings on a regular basis, and the mothers worked for the schools in voluntary capacities, assisting in libraries, producing flyers, taking part in safety programs, and working as members of the various committees of the parent associations. Within this framework they mediated their children's school experiences of learning to read and write.

Negotiating the Present in Light of the Past

Recollections of the past gained meaning in the present as the parents negotiated their children's early school experiences. Most of the parents spoke of their first-grade year as an unsettling time for them, and they portrayed it as such for their children. Barry Lindell spoke of the difficult move that Sandy had made from kindergarten to first grade, while Karen Farley commented at the end of Kathy's first-grade year that there were times when she could have cried because dealing with Kathy was so difficult. Nina Simms expressed the problem in terms of the work that first-grade children are expected to do; she said, "They're expected to read, they're expected to write, and they're expected to do math. It's a lot and too much for some kids." Other parents spoke of the length of the day and the amount of time the children were expected to sit. First grade was portrayed by the parents as a period of transition. New schedules, new rules, and new work were a part of the school situation with which the first grader had to contend. While it was a new experience for the child, it was a familiar experience for the parents. It had happened to them in their own childhoods, and for some it had happened more recently through the experiences of their older children.

Parents spoke of their children's experiences within the context of their own experience. This is well illustrated by Leo Langdon's comments on the discussion he had with Jill when they were deciding on a school for Ken. He said they had discussed sending Ken to a parochial school, but because of his experience and because Jill had gone to a public school, they had decided against it. Leo emphasized, "I did not particularly want to send my child to a parochial school because of the experiences I had." As Ken entered first grade, Leo and Jill continued their discussion. On one occasion, Jill spoke specifically of reading. She explained:

> My husband and I have been talking about this a lot now because we are starting in with this with Ken. I don't remember how we started but I can remember once we knew some words and could read the "Dick and Jane" books; I can remember going around the room and everybody reading a sentence from the book. That I can remember. And one thing we've been talking about is right now the way our schools are set up the children are placed in levels because it's the Ginn method of reading, and my husband doesn't really think that this whole level thing is good. He feels it makes the child feel that there's someone else smarter than they are or they're behind. I said that when I was in first grade I could remember we knew who was not reading because we would have this reading a sentence and it would always be the same person who would stumble on words so I said I didn't think that was right either because that makes that person feel awful.

Leo also spoke of this issue commenting, "It just upset me that they were putting pressure on the children." The situation was complicated for Leo and Jill by the school's insistence that the children in Ken's first-grade year participate in a series of reading tests which were being given throughout the school. The children had spent two weeks in first grade when they were tested. Ken came home upset. Leo recalled:

> He was upset that he couldn't read the instructions and couldn't read the words he was supposed to read to get the right answers and I immediately became upset about it because I told him he didn't have to know how to read yet, he was only in the first grade for the second week and that he shouldn't be upset about it and he got over that.

In mediating Ken's early experiences of reading in first grade, Leo and Jill worked to minimize the pressure they felt was being exerted within the school situation. They faced a specific problem, and in so doing they combined their personal experiences as they searched for some way of easing Ken into his first-grade year. They had established a home environment for Ken and Steven in which the children were not pushed toward academic activities. Of reading, Jill had commented that they read stories "to enjoy now, not to pressure them into anything else." But the pressure had come, and they had an urgent need to deal with it. Leo explained to Ken that it was OK that he was not reading in his second week of first grade, while Jill down-played the idea of levels, emphasizing that it did not matter which level you were in as long as you were working. The Langdon parents spent an anxious few weeks as Ken got deeper into first grade. Ken started to read. He was reading well. That Christmas Leo commented,

> But I'm amazed today, Ken comes home with books and he can actually read the books, actually read them and I'm so impressed because I can remember when I was in first grade I could not read a book. He's motivated to read, he wants to read.

Teaching in School and Learning at Home

Within the context of the family, the transmission of literary styles and values is a diffuse experience, often occurring at the margins of awareness. Even when parents quite consciously introduced their children to print, the words were locked into the context of the situation. The label on the shampoo bottle, the recipe for carrot bread, and the neon signs in the street were not constructed to specifically teach reading; they were part of the child's world, and the child learned of their purpose as well as of their meaning. However, the data also indicate that "shifts" occurred in the parents' approaches to the transmission of literacy styles and values, and these shifts coincided with the child's beginning to learn to read and write in school. Leo and Jill Langdon had not consciously tried to teach their children to read, but in the middle of Ken's first-grade year, it became clear that he was learning to read without difficulty. He was inter-ested in words; he was inquisitive about the words in his own home. At that time Leo and Jill began to participate in his reading activities. He explained, "A couple of months ago I went over to see his teacher and I had spoken to her and told her how well he was doing, how we felt. I asked her if he could bring books home so that we could help him and he could read and she said 'sure.' " Ken took home the books and read them to his family and Leo decided to ask for more. Jill listens to him read whenever she can, and Leo helps him read words and sentences out of the magazines in their home. Ken is motivated to learn, and Leo and Jill are determined to help him while they continue to downplay the competition at school.

The active role that the child plays in bringing specific written language activities into the home was noted in each of the families.

Sensitive to the child's response to school-related activities, the parents joined with the child in incorporating them into the life of the family. Like Ken Langdon, the Lindell children demonstrated their interest in written language. The Lindells spoke of the times when their children had become interested in words. Laura and Barry had played word games with their children during their kindergarten and first-grade years. Laura spoke of the children coming home from school and wanting to play with words. Barry created word games to play with them. Speaking of one game he had played with Sandy, he said, "Fill-in-the-blank-space type thing; that helps an awful lot and in fact it becomes addictive. We'll play it for hours." Now, Sandy is in third grade and no longer interested in such games. Both Laura and Barry have emphasized that they played these games spasmodically, depending on the interest of the children. Laura explained that so much of it had come from them, and she added, "It's like everything else; sometimes in your life you'll do something very intensively, like for a couple of weeks, and maybe not at all for a long time."

THE INFLUENCE OF THE OLDER CHILDREN'S SCHOOL EXPERIENCES ON THEIR YOUNGER SIBLINGS

The experiences of the older children reflect upon and, in some ways, shape the experiences of the younger children. While parents spoke of spending less time with their younger children, they also spoke of trying to provide them with experiences which they had not given their older children. Jill Langdon spoke of teaching Steven to differentiate between left and right because Ken had been expected to understand these concepts when he had entered first grade; Donna King spoke of teaching James his address and telephone number as Bonnie had been expected to know this information when she began school. This was not confined to the younger children's preschool years; their parents continued to mediate their experiences in light of those of their older siblings. Laura Lindell said that she was much more prepared to intervene for Sandy than she had been for Sarah and Beth. Laura did intervene for Sandy. Sandy had been in first grade for two weeks when Laura went to see the teacher. Laura explained that Sandy was bored with all the "getting to know each other" activities of the first two weeks. Laura asked the teacher to give Sandy some work that was in keeping with what she had been doing at the end of her kindergarten year.

The older children also influence the experiences of their young siblings more directly. From simple exposure to the activities of their older brothers and sisters, school is a part of the climate in which the younger children grow. School is a part of the family life, and it shapes the lives of younger children in ways their older siblings missed. Leo Langdon spoke of Steven being present when Ken was reading to them during his first-grade year. He stated, "He's there, he hears it, it's going on." Donna King talked of Bonnie playing with James, showing him how to write letters while they were playing. She commented that Bonnie had focused on letters that were possibly easier to form, such as H, A, and E, rather than working through the alphabet. Karen Farley spoke of Kathy doing more interesting things with Debbie, and she emphasized that in these games Kathy was able to share with Debbie many school-related literate experiences that would have smacked of teaching if she (Karen) had attempted them. Debbie demonstrated her awareness of Kathy's school activities several times, speaking of the homework Kathy brought home from school. Once Debbie explained that Kathy had to write something about the news she had watched on television. I asked Debbie if she had helped Kathy with her homework. She replied she had not, and then she added as an afterthought, "But I watched!" Perhaps it was Debbie's awareness of her sister's homework that led her to speak of her own writing activities as homework, for every afternoon before her nap Debbie would sit at the desk in her bedroom practicing the letters of the alphabet in a book Karen had bought for her. Ellie Dawson also watched. Both Sissie and Hannah talked of Ellie joining them in their rooms when they did their homework. Ellie would draw while they worked.

CONCLUSIONS

In his 1925 Lowell Lectures, Alfred North Whitehead stated, "mere change without conservation is a passage from nothing to nothing," while "conservation without change cannot conserve. For after all, there is a flux of circumstance, and the freshness of being evaporates under mere repetition." This is the essence of my interpretation.

Neisser, writing of memory, states, "Much of that formative past is now tacit rather than explicit knowledge: I do not dwell on it, and I cannot recall it as such, the specifics are beyond recall, although their resultant is here in person" (1979, p. 13). In the ongoing dialogue with the families, I was continuously impressed by the way the parents' interpretations of the present were bound by their recollections of the past. The conservation of past literate experiences was noted in the many implicit linkages between the past and present, as parents spoke of their childhood experiences and then later described similar experiences they had shared with their children. Implicit linking was also evidenced in the reading of stories, as some of the parents found that the stories they shared with their children were stories they had listened to when they were young.

In addition to the implicit linking of the past with the present, many ties were made directly as the memories of the parents were juxtaposed with the present-day experiences of the children. On such occasions, the parents were deliberately intent upon providing alternate experiences for their children. Dewey defines such deliberations as designed "to resolve entanglements in existing activity, restore continuity, recover harmony, utilize loose impulse and redirect habit," and he goes on to state, "Deliberation has its beginning in troubled activity and its conclusion in choice of a course of action which straightens it out" (1922, p. 187). In considering the present data, when the parents were intent on change, the course of action they chose was closely related to their need to provide for their children experiences they had missed. Thus the interplay of the individual biographies and educative styles of the parents becomes the dominant factor in shaping the literate experiences of the children within the home. And yet, from the very beginning, the children are active and reactive in the sharing of literate experiences with their parents. Dewey speaks of the continuous alteration of such patterns by children as "unconscious and unintended." He speaks of immature and undeveloped activity succeeding in modifying "adult organized activity accidently and surreptitiously" (p. 92). Undoubtedly, each child brings a new dimension to the transmission of literacy style and values within the family.

3

Family Literacy and the Social Organization of Everyday Life

The clarity of language is not behind it in a universal grammar we may carry upon our person; it is before language, in what the infinitesimal gestures of any scrawling on the paper or each vocal inflection reveals to the horizon as their meaning. (Merleau-Ponty, 1973, p. 28)

In the early stages of the study, the extent of the children's literate activity was only hinted at in the ongoing dialogue with each family. Reading and writing are so much a part of the lives of these parents and children that their experiences are too diffuse for casual commentary. New strategies of data collection were necessary if the degree of their involvement was to be made visible. My dilemma was partly resolved by Nina Simms when she took me on a literacy search of her home. This approach was adopted with each of the families, and it proved especially useful with the children, since the print in their homes provides a tangible basis for discussion. Another approach that proved equally fruitful was collecting examples of the writings (e.g., notes, lists, and letters) of both the parents and the children. I often noticed such artifacts when visiting the families, and I invariably asked if I could have them for my research. Sometimes the papers were too precious for the families to part with, and so I borrowed them to copy; at other times, the papers were already in the garbage, and my interest was viewed with skepticism as the items were considered of little value. This in itself was considered of importance to the research, and again, the discussions which the artifacts stimulated proved an invaluable source of information. In addition, opportunities arose to observe the children interacting with and through print while playing with their friends, and many examples of their writings were retrieved, crumpled and torn, from the street or the garbage where they lay discarded.

In chapter 2, the transmission of literacy styles and values was viewed as a social process in which the reading and writing experiences of the children are mediated by the individual members of the families; in this chapter, literacy is viewed, on another level, as a filter through which the social organization of the everyday lives of the families is accomplished. The children, as integral members of the social organization, use print as one medium through which they can master their surroundings. It enables them to build new social connections as well as to establish new environmental relationships, and the meanings of print are before them in their inventive constructions of literacy in their daily activities.

LITERACY AND EVERYDAY LIFE

In the early stages of the research, the parents and children spoke of what they usually read and write in an average day. Their many comments formed the basis of an ongoing dialogue which led to the exploration of literacy as one means the family had of mediating its experiences of one another.

Parents: Reading and Writing

In each of the families, literacy facilitates the accomplishment of many essential daily tasks and is a critical factor in the continuation of present lifestyles. Each parent employed outside of the home depends upon his or her ability to process print to fulfill his or her job requirements. Joe King spends much of his day reading the masses of paperwork which is the administrator's lot, while Leo Langdon spends his working day processing legal claims for an engineering company. Jessie Dawson reads stories she will eventually share with the children in the school library where she works, and in the early stages of the study she was fulfilling the literate tasks of a legal secretary. Nina Simms, in her job as a Tupperware representative, is involved in organizing parties and in the form-filling tasks of ordering Tupperware products. Literate pursuits are an integral part of the working routine, and sometimes, as in the case of Laura Lindell who is becoming a writer, reading and writing are the routine. In a letter to me Laura wrote, "I am now on page 20 and need a closing final wrap-up paragraph. . . . But it is 4:30 and I've been at it since 9:30 so I need a diversion." Laura often spends her entire working day at her typewriter. At the time Laura wrote this letter, she was spending most of her time writing, but during the three years of the study she has worked in various capacities. She has been a substitute teacher and is presently a technician in Barry's laboratory at the university.

The parents also spoke of the many literate tasks necessary to the smooth running of the home. From the completion of income tax forms to the sorting out of junk mail, literacy is an essential ingredient of family life. However, there is great variation in the ways these tasks are accomplished. For example, Laura and Barry Lindell work on their tax forms together. Jessie and Dan Dawson and Nina and Azar Simms, however, employ accountants to set their records straight, but the preparation of the relevant information is still a time-consuming chore. With junk mail, there is similar variation. Karen Farley stands by the kitchen garbage container, systematically sorting and discarding the daily mail. Jill Langdon sorts through the mail, keeping the advertisements, such as magazine subscription offers, so she can give the stamps they often contain to Ken and Steven. Nina Simms, speaking of junk mail, commented, "Half of it I keep," and laughing she added, "because it's junk." Nina explained that she often kept advertisements with the intention of sending away for the products they offered, but that after about a year she would find that the expiration date of the offer had passed, and then she would throw the literature away.

Keeping financial records and even sorting junk mail are obligatory tasks. The state and federal governments require income tax returns each year, and income tax evasion results in court action. The disregard of junk mail would not result in such a dilemma, but because it arrives on a continuing basis, some action has to be taken.

With other literate pursuits, such as reading newspapers, there is an element of choice. Most of the parents spoke of reading multiple newspapers on a daily basis. Azar Simms buys two newspapers every morning and reads them while commuting to the office. In the evening, he buys another paper to read on the way home. He then gives the three papers to Nina who reads them in the evening. The parents' comments about newspaper reading indicate that they have evolved individual styles for dealing with the masses of print which confront them on every page. Lee Farley described his reading of the *Wall Street Journal*. He stated:

> If I'm lucky I can get the entire paper done between the time I get on the bus and the time I hit the office. Everything. I mean there'll be a few screwball articles I have no interest in reading . . . but I try to kill it totally . . . I think I can do it right down to the editorials, the reviews, the whole shmeer . . . But if I hit an article which has a lot of numerical information in it, or graphs, histories . . . and you know you're trying to remember all this. . . then it slows you down.

Lee reads the *Wall Street Journal* for the information it contains and because he enjoys the paper. It is a good way to pass the time while traveling on the bus. Laura Lindell reads newspapers for other reasons, and her description of her approach to the reading of the Sunday *New York Times* reflects these differences. She explained:

> We get the *New York Times* on Sunday. I dutifully try to read some of it, and most always I get so disgusted with the state of the world that I read lots of the headlines and decide that this is all too depressing. I read a few articles in the Sunday *Magazine* and I read a few articles in the *Book Review*.

If there are variations in the approaches of the parents to such reading, there are similarities in the ritualistic ways in which they read. Newspapers are a part of the daily routine. They are read at certain times in specific places. Reading on the bus or while a preschool child naps is part of the ritual.

In December 1978, the *New York Times* strike was the main topic of conversation at the Dawsons' Christmas party. The discussion centered on the difficulties of keeping up with current affairs without a good newspaper. There was a lot of teasing about the effect on the family when Dad cannot read the newspaper at the breakfast table; Jessie, laughing, said the strike had almost ended their marriage. Dan Dawson spends half an hour each day at the breakfast table reading the *New York Times*. But half an hour is insufficient time for him to read the entire paper, and so it is eventually placed with the unread magazines and papers stacked at the right of his chair. On the floor to the left of his chair is another pile of papers and magazines; these Dan has read. Neither pile seems to decrease, and both piles are creeping up to the top of the arms of the chair.

On reading books, the comments of the parents were mixed. Lee Farley spoke of himself as a "complete illiterate," and he explained that the last novel he read was during his stay in the hospital following an emergency appendectomy. Lee said it was either that or daytime television, and he had chosen to read a book. However, some months later the Farleys bought a sailboat, and Lee was reading more books. One Saturday morning, I saw Lee sitting on the garage floor with a book of nautical knots in front of him. About this time, Karen spoke of the massive text on sailing that Lee was reading on his way to work every morning. Joe King described himself in a similar fashion to Lee. He said he was "not a reader," and that the only books he read were about American history and tennis. Joe spoke of what he called "should reading" and went on to state:

Since graduate school I've always had a list of books I should read. OK, so in graduate school I should read these psychology books or whatever it was. In my profession, I should read these books to keep up and I never seem to get around to should reading.

Perhaps Dan Dawson would fit the definition that Joe might give of "a reader." Dan spoke of reading three novels a week from the library. He described how he often wakes at 4:30 in the morning to read, and noting my surprise, he continued, "Yes, for the fun of it." The rest of the parents read novels spasmodically. Jill Langdon commented that there were long periods when she did not read, but if she found a book she liked, she would read it at every opportunity. She said, "I read it when I'm cooking, read it until it's finished. *Coma* or something like that, the kind of book you can't put down." Both Karen Farley and Donna King spoke of a similar compulsiveness in their reading of novels, and they too emphasized that there were long periods when they did not read fiction. Laura Lindell also reads spasmodically and enjoys her children's books as well as adult fiction. Barry Lindell has little time for fiction, and he emphasized that he has difficulty keeping up with the many journals in his field. However, Laura sometimes gives him a chapter-by-chapter, blow-by-blow account of the books that she reads. On one occasion, she spoke of sharing with Barry the novel *Wifey* by Judy Blume. Laura explained that she had read the "juicy bits" to Barry and the descriptions of the policemen which were so funny because they reminded them of the policemen in their own town.

Conversations with the parents provided some information of what they write in their daily lives. Clearly, writing plays an important role in many tasks both at work and at home. In each of the families, events were noted on an engagement calendar kept near the telephone in the kitchen, and important telephone numbers and notices, such as information about school events, were displayed on either a notice board or the refrigerator. As previously mentioned, form filling was portrayed as an endless task, with record keeping considered a necessary chore. Few of the parents took as much pleasure in writing as they did in reading such things as newspapers and novels. They wrote few letters. Instead, salutations to family and friends were quickly sent on cards purchased for that purpose, or simply were not sent at all. Azar Simms spoke with regret of losing touch with his family because he no longer wrote the twenty-page epistles that he had written for so many years. Jessie Dawson also spoke of the days when she had more time to write to her family and friends, and she commented that all there was time for these days was a quick phone call. Laura Lindell dislikes the phone and often ignores it when it rings. Telephoning her family and friends is no solution, and she prefers to write letters. One letter that she wrote began, "It seems ridiculous to phone when I have this glorious machine which spits out my thoughts for me." So even though Laura sends letters, they are often typed rather than handwritten.

Children: Reading and Writing

Many of the children participating in the research are of school age, and, as with their parents in the work place, their ability to process print facilitates the fulfillment of many school requirements. At the beginning of the study many of the children were learning to read in school; now they have joined their older siblings in reading to learn. Sandy Lindell had just entered first grade and was learning to read when she began to participate in the study. At the conclusion of the study she was a third grader, and reading was required for the work she brought home from school. One of her assignments began with the directions, "Answer the questions below. You will need a dictionary or an encyclopedia to help you."

In addition to the obligatory tasks of completing school assignments, reading has become an integral part of the daily lives of the older children. The clear account of twelve-year-old Beth Lindell of what she read in an average day showed this involvement. Beth said that she read "everything." When she awoke in the morning, she tried to finish the chapter she had been reading the previous night. At the breakfast table, she read the cereal boxes and the milk carton. Once on the school bus, there were license plates and mailboxes, but Beth added that this usually did not work as the bus went too fast. At school, she read "all those books." After school, she played with her friends, and there were always new T-shirts to read. Beth said that sometimes when she came in, she would make a cake, reading the directions on the box of cake mix. After dinner she did her homework, and she continued mischievously by saying that once it was finished, she would "sneak down and get outside" to play again before bedtime. When bedtime finally came, she would once again read a book.

The younger children in each of the families listen to stories read by their parents at bedtime. Interestingly, in each family, the child who was learning to read at the time that the family agreed to participate in the study is still listening to stories. Nina Simms reads to Andrew each night at bedtime, and Carol joins in the occasion which has been part of her daily routine since she was a baby. Ken and Steven Langdon listen together to stories that Jill reads, and Kathy Farley listens to the stories that Karen reads to Debbie and Nan before she settles in her own bed to read to herself. Ellie Dawson is nine years of age and still listens to the stories that Jessie reads. Jessie has been reading to her children since Sissie was a baby nineteen years ago, and she still enjoys the ritual. She gets into bed beside Ellie and, propped up with pillows, they share the stories.

In addition to reading stories, many of the children read magazines which they receive on a regular basis. Many of the subscriptions are given to the children as birthday presents, and the choice of the magazine changes as they grow older. Bonnie King received the *Sesame Street Magazine* in her preschool years, followed by *Ranger Rick* and the *Electric Company Magazine*. At the present time, Bonnie is eight years of age, and she receives *World Magazine*; her mother is talking of subscribing to *Sesame Street Magazine* again, only this time the magazine would be for James.

In each of the families, the children draw pictures and write on a daily basis. Carol Simms keeps the names of her friends and their telephone numbers near the telephone in the kitchen, while Ellie Dawson writes down important events such as ballet lessons and birthday parties on the calendar in her room. Ken Langdon has a large looseleaf folder in which he jots down his homework assignments and draws the tanks, destroyers, and space ships of his battles on earth and in space. Sandy Lindell writes notes to herself. Once when she had forgotten to take home a birthday invitation, she wrote on a torn piece of paper, "Sandy take home Vicki's card." She left this note on the top of her desk where she would see it when it was time to go home. Bonnie King also writes messages to herself, especially when she must take things to school such as a plastic bag of clay. Bonnie pinned a note to her notice board to help her remember the bag. The work of Bonnie and James King fills boxes which Donna stores in the basement, and their current work is taped to the walls in the dining room and to the door of the refrigerator. The pictures of Andrew Simms, complete with his name, are hung in the kitchen by Nina and Andrew. Nina once commented, "If he can find a space he'll hang a picture." The literate endeavors of Carol fill the drawers of the cupboard in the dining room and the desk in the family room. They are constantly threatening to invade the floor. Nina said she found it difficult to keep up with the proliferation of paper and she often tossed out the old scraps of paper that were left lying around at the end of the day.

Despite many conversations about writing, much was left unsaid; the families' writing activities were too diffuse to tap in such a casual manner. Jill Langdon noted this problem when I asked her if I could look at the small notebook that I had seen when Ken had opened a kitchen drawer. The book appeared to belong to the children as it was open at a page where Steven had written his name. Jill gave me the notebook, and together we looked through it, stopping at a list which was written on one of the pages. Jill could not remember when the list had been written, and only when she discussed it with Ken did she remember the occasion. She commented afterwards that it was hard to remember the times when such writing was done and added that so much was done without her knowledge, only to be tossed into some drawer or into the garbage once it had outlived its usefulness. Undoubtedly, Jill is right, and information about such writing is difficult to retrieve. But as the research proceeded, many such artifacts were collected, and, in most instances, both parents and children could describe the circumstances of their being written.

LITERACY AND THE MEDIATION OF EXPERIENCE

The children in this study are surrounded by the print of their parents; it is part of their environment. On one tour of his home, Ken Langdon showed me the book *People of the Lake: Mankind and Its Beginning* by Richard Leakey and Roger Lewin, which he said that his father was reading. On a similar occasion, Ellie Dawson, having showed me the piles of papers on each side of her father's chair, stopped at her mother's desk and, pointing to the disarray of papers, explained that even though it looked messy, they never touched them because her mother knew exactly where everything was located. But the children do more than see their parents read or engage in literate activities, for with their parents they share the experience of print in mediating their relationships.

Parents and Children Communicating through the Medium of Print

Each of the families writes notes. Hill and Varenne (1979) point out that any understanding of family conversations must "begin with the ongoing social situation in which the communication is embedded" (p. 49). In a similar way, any understanding of the notes' messages depends on an appreciation of the ways they were embedded in the context of family life. The data show that the parents write messages to one another when the information cannot be delivered directly. Dan Dawson was called away on business after Jessie had left for work, and so he left a note for her on the kitchen table. It stated where he was going and how long he would be away, and tacked on the bottom of the note was the postscript, "I've found my underwear." Jessie explained that she had come downstairs one morning to find Dan standing in front of the dryer waiting for his underwear. Jessie had washed the clothes the day before but had forgotten to put them in the dryer. Another such note was written by Barry Lindell to Laura. Barry left the note in the kitchen where Laura would see it when she came home. It read:

> Laura—I ate pizza—rest on stove.
> Margaret called again—wants to talk with
> you. Dog gone when I got home. Put him on
> chain if he arrives before you go out again.
> See you at—6:00. Will jog first. Barry.

Added to the note was the postscript, "Snowdrops are up!" Before the winter, Laura and Barry had planted some snowdrop bulbs, and this was the first sighting of the young plants.

In each of the families, parents wrote notes to their children. However, most of these notes were written by the mothers, and the degree to which such note writing took place was dependent on a variety of factors. Nina Simms explained that while her children were young, there was seldom an occasion that warranted leaving a message. Karen Farley maintained a similar position, writing notes only when she could not speak to her children directly. One such note Karen had left taped to her front door. It read:

> Dear Kathy and Debbie,
> Please be very quiet—Nan is sleeping.
> Thank you.
>
> > Love, Mommy

Kathy was seven years of age and Debbie was four years and two months at the time that Karen posted the note. They had been to lunch at my house and had arrived home after Nan had been put to bed for her afternoon nap.

The Lindell children are older, and with their busy schedules they are seldom in the same place at the same time. The Lindells' reliance on written messages has greatly increased during the three years of the study. The children's schedules are more complex, and writing lists, memos, and notes is one way the family keeps on top of their busy lives. Laura Lindell commented that so much was always happening that sometimes if she did not write a note, she would forget what it was she wanted to say to her children. One such note stated:

> Beth—Don't forget your violin Friday—
> take a small hand towel for a chin rest.

Laura wrote this note on Thursday evening after Beth had gone to bed. She put it on the kitchen table so Beth would find it when she had her breakfast. Laura used this note as an example of information that would have been lost if it had not been written down. She said, "I'd never have remembered to remind her in the morning." Laura also writes notes that require answers. One note that Laura wrote to Sandy asked if she would like to iron some hand towels. Other notes that the Lindell parents write are more cryptic and meant for all the children, like the one in the bathroom which bans showers before school because Sarah had left for school one winter morning with wet hair after a shower, or the one on the front door which Barry had written after the door had been slammed one time too many. It read, "Please do not slam this door. It really works."

Donna King works several afternoons a week, and as she is not home when Bonnie arrives from school, she sometimes leaves notes for her. Some of her notes also require answers. One day Donna bought Bonnie a headband, and as she was at work when Bonnie came home, she left it on Bonnie's bed with a note. In the note, she asked Bonnie if she liked the headband, explaining that if she did not, they could take it back to the store. Bonnie, in turn, replied:

> Dear Mommy,
> I love the headband. Thank you.
> Love Bonnie

She taped the note to the door of her mother's bedroom to make sure that she would see it when she came home from work.

The children write to their parents for a variety of reasons. From dedications on drawings and salutations on homemade cards to informational notations, they are using print to communicate with their parents. Andrew Simms at four years and ten months practiced writing his numbers and then asked Carol, his older sister, to write the message, "To the whole family from Andrew." Andrew then copied the dedication and gave the page of numbers to his mother. At Thanksgiving, when Debbie Farley was four years and eleven months, she drew a smiling person and wrote, "DEARMOMDEBBIE I AM SENDING A CARD." Debbie was at her grandmother's celebrating Thanksgiving, but her mother had stayed home because she was ill. Karen said that she thought Debbie had written "DEARMOM-DEBBIE" by herself and then had asked one of the adults at the party to spell "I AM SENDING A CARD." In a similar manner, Ken at seven years and six months had sent a get well present to his mother. Ken and his cousin Mike wrapped some modeling clay in paper and attached a note to it. They wrote, "get well!! from Ken," and "get well from Ken and Mike."

Bonnie King at seven years and seven months left the message in Figure 3.1 for her mother to find when she returned from work (see p. 36). The letter was unsigned. Donna said she felt Bonnie had written the note because she had wanted to tell Donna about her day. At about this time, Bonnie wrote another letter to Donna in which she said:

> Dear Mommie,
> I really love you. Yes I do.
> You care for me. And I know
> why you tell me to have
> gum olny every other day
> I know it all. It is for my
> own good. So I don't get
> cavities you are the mother
> I want for ever
> and ever.   Love Bonnie
>   x x x x   o o o o o o ø
>   x x x x   o o o o o o ø
>   x x x x
>   I love you

Donna explained that she felt Bonnie had left the note for her because she knew Donna was feeling a little unhappy. That morning, Bonnie had asked Donna what was wrong, and Donna had told her that she was "feeling down." Donna added that the remarks Bonnie had made about the gum amused her because they had talked about having too much gum a few days before, but in the context of the letter it seemed that Bonnie had included it because she wanted something to say between the "I love you's."

There were other kinds of letters written by the children to their parents. Jessie Dawson spoke of the notes Hannah had written to Dan since she was a little girl. She wrote them at bedtime and left them in

Dear Mom,
I put it on channel 3
and seseame street was
on. Then I put channel
8 on and there
was Mr. Rogers!
there's some on the back

I had a good time
at Jack's house. We went
to Froggy Park. I love
you very much. Can you give
me a kiss when you come
home.

Fig. 3.1

her parents' room. Jessie said that they usually contained requests for such things as an early morning call so Hannah could finish her homework, but very often Hannah added other requests which she found it easier to write than to ask for in person. Nina Simms also talked of the letters of request that Carol wrote. One of these letters stated:

> To Mom
> Please let me
> stay up because
> if i don't see the
> program now, I will
> never get the
> chance to see it.
> it's now or *never*
> yes no
> circle
> yes

Carol had been watching a television special, and it was past her bedtime, so Nina sent her to bed. Carol wrote the note in her room and took it downstairs to her mother. Nina let her watch the conclusion of the program in her bedroom. She told Carol to keep the sound down because Azar did not know that she was still awake.

During the course of the study, I talked with many parents about the writing endeavors of their children. Several parents spoke of their children writing letters of complaint about their siblings, and one mother told me of the "I hate you" notes that her daughter wrote and left on her mother's pillow for her to find when she went to bed.

I also paid attention to the notes that my own children wrote. Among the many notes I collected were the following: "Dear Mummy and Daddy my head hurts love Ben"; "Dear Louise I don't want to be your friend"; and "Dear Mummy and Daddy, I hate to tattletale But I just couldn't help it! BENJAMIN put Aim tooth past on the off wite Rug in the hall so people will step in it! It is one in. and 3 senameters! I almost steped in it. It felt gwee! It is near the green rug. You daughter Louise Taylor." (See Figure 3.2.)

Read

Mummy & Daddy

Dear Mummy & Daddy,
        I hate to tatletalie
But I just coulded help it!
            BENJAMIN
Put Aimtooth Past on the off-wite
Rud So pepole in the Hall will
step in it!   it is one in. and   3

senameters? I Almost speped in it.

        it felf gwee!
it is nere the Green rug.

            your Daghter,
                Louise Taylor

Fig. 3.2

ESTABLISHING NEW SOCIAL CONNECTIONS
AND ENVIRONMENTAL RELATIONSHIPS
THROUGH THE MEDIUM OF PRINT

Dewey (1922) states, "all conduct is interaction between elements of human nature and the environment, natural and social" (p. 11). The children were using print on many levels in their daily lives. Writing lists and personal memos was one of the ways they reminded themselves of tasks to be accomplished and social events to be attended. Writing letters and making registers of club members sometimes facilitated transactions between siblings and friends; and things such as signs and computer data cards were used to explore the complex environment.

Siblings and Friends
Establishing Social Connections through the Use of Print
Siblings and friends often used print in the social accomplishment of their daily activities. It was one means of forging links and of effecting the social organization of group activities.

When James King was hospitalized with a bronchial infection, Bonnie and her friend Fran sent him letters to cheer him up. Bonnie wrote, "I hope you are feeling better." On the fourth birthday of Andrew Simms, Carol, who was then six years and two months, sent him a card. She wrote his name fifty-two times on the envelope, and on the inside of the card, she wrote, "To my big brother your so very fine." Ellie Dawson writes short letters to her sister Sissie, who is now at college, and encloses pictures she has drawn. In one letter Ellie sent Sissie a picture of a tree, which Sissie pinned in the center of her notice board. Ellie also writes letters to her friends. When she was nine years and one month she wrote to Kathy Farley telling her about her vacation. Ellie wrote:

PAGE ONE
Dear Kathy
        I'm taking rideing
rideing lessons and
sailing lessons I
really like rideing
because the horse
that I ride with
(blaze is the name
riding's the game.) Is

a very good horse.
　　　when you have a
rideing lesson you
have to be wareing
certain things
if you're not you
can't ride. the list
is on the other
page
　　　PAGE TWO
jodfers—pants—tight
hat—black—hard
boots—steel toe
　　　the lesson
the first thing we
do in rideing class is to
walk around the ring
then we start to
trot around the ring
the last thing we
do is get of the
horse.

Ellie did not sign the letter, but Kathy knew who it was from, and Karen Farley spoke of how pleased Kathy was to hear from her friend. Some eight months later Kathy still had the letter in her desk, although she had thrown away many other papers. Similarly, for many months Bonnie King had a letter from a friend pinned to her notice board. The note stated:

Dear Bonnie,
I like you very
much.
From Kelly

It was not only the older children who communicated with one another through print. When Debbie Farley was three years and six months of age, she sent a birthday greeting to Hannah Dawson (see Figure 3.3). It was written on a piece of note paper which sported the greeting "Hello" at the top of the page. Debbie drew a daisy and a yellow and purple sun. Above the daisy, she copied the salutation

Fig. 3.3

"Hello" in purple crayon. One year later, Hannah still had Debbie's daisy pinned to the notice board in her bedroom.

Read (1975) has written of preschool children and their early writing endeavors. Read writes that very often context and spelling can be used to identify the words which were intended. However,

Read presents a different perspective than the one considered here.
He states of the children's writings:

> Their functional utility is dubious; frequently the addressee, if
> there was one, could not read the message. Sometimes, at the
> early stages, the writer himself could not read what he had
> written after a day or two had passed. Clearly, some of the
> children began to write before they could read, in the usual
> sense. In that respect, this is a case of production preceding
> comprehension. (p. 330)

My findings indicate that it is not production that precedes comprehension but use that precedes form, or as Cazden (1980) states,
performance that precedes competence. The children explored the
uses of print before they learned specifically of the form of written
language. When Steven was three years and six months of age, he sent
a letter to his friend Andrew Simms. Steven sealed the envelope
without showing his mother what he had written. He then asked her
to address the envelope, and together they took the letter to the post
office. When I asked Nina Simms about the letter that Andrew had
received from Steven, she described his reaction. She said Andrew
was really pleased to receive a letter, and when she had asked him if he
understood what Steven had written, he had replied "of course."
Nina could not find the letter, but she described it as a page of circles
with lines through them. When Steven was four years and three
months, he wrote Andrew another letter. This time he wrote his
name four times on a piece of yellow lined paper, and once again, he
posted it with his mother. Steven did not continue writing letters;
however, he has been the recipient of letters from friends that have
moved away from his neighborhood. Fifteen months after Steven
wrote to Andrew, he has received a reply. Andrew (five years and six
months) has sent a letter to Steven. He wrote "Steven" and then
"Andrew" on a piece of paper; with Nina he put it in an envelope
which she addressed, and together they took it to the post office.

The children often used print while playing with their friends.
Forming clubs was a significant aspect of their play. Even Nan
Farley, at the age of two, played with her sisters in Ellie Dawson's
clubhouse. Many of the arrangements the children made in organizing their clubs were committed to paper. However, such writings
were particularly difficult to obtain. Several of the papers included in
this study were found in the street where they had been discarded,
while others were too private to share. Beth Lindell told me of the
clubs she had formed with her sister Sarah and her friends. One of

these clubs she referred to as the Ghost Club. Beth explained that they each had a spirit, and as part of their commitment to the club, each member had to write "the whole history of the spirit's life." I expressed my interest in what they had written, and Beth asked Sarah, who was the president of the club, if I could see the book in which they had written. Sarah said that as her friends had also written in the book, she felt it would be unfair to show it to me. Sarah's reluctance to show me the book raised the issue of the participants' right to privacy. It was clear from the way that Sarah answered my queries that she really did not want to show me the book. Obtaining the data would have been a violation of privacy; thus I did not ask for it again.

The younger children seemed interested in writing down more practical information. Jill Langdon expressed it well when she commented on the writing which interested Ken and his friends when they formed clubs. She stated, "Mostly what they write is who's in and who's out."

In the spring of 1979, Ellie Dawson cleaned out the old tin shed in her yard while playing with a neighbor's visiting granddaughter. Once the young visitor had left, Ellie asked Kathy Farley, Debbie Farley, and Louise Taylor, my daughter, to join her club. Their immediate concern was, as Jill Langdon had observed of the club activities of Ken and his friends, for "who's in and who's out." On one piece of paper, Ellie wrote with a thick black marker:

The Club Members

Kathy Farley	Ellie Dawson
Louise Taylor	Lucy Farley
Debbie Farley	

Underneath, two names had been obliterated with thick black ink. They were the names of Ben Taylor and his friend Seth Morrison who had joined the group for a short while before deciding to spend their time spying on the activities of the club rather than joining in. (Lucy is the Farley's dog.)

Membership in the club was constantly renegotiated, with each of the children excluded at one time or another. On one occasion, while Kathy Farley was away for the day with her family, Ellie and Louise wrote her a note. With an old knife from the Dawson's kitchen they fashioned a pen and, making mud ink out of dirt and water, they wrote:

> Dear Kathy
>   You are
> fired from
> the club!
> from
> Louise
> and Ellie

The following day, Louise showed Kathy Farley how to make stick pens and mud ink. Several days later, Kathy showed Debbie, her younger sister.

Although the negotiations were often volatile and other clubs, including the Preteen Sweethearts Club, were formed, Ellie's club endured. Perhaps part of the secret of its success was the old tin shed, for club members spent much of their time arranging to take care of it, and it was within this context that they constantly renegotiated their social arrangements. For some time, the children wrote on a blackboard which they hid behind the shed. Each time the children played at the clubhouse, they wrote on the blackboard the tasks that each member would complete. The tasks ranged from watering the flowers to rearranging the clubhouse furniture. When they finished playing, the writing was erased.

Toward the end of the summer, the children were given some straw board by Lee Farley who was clearing out his garage. Each child used the straw board to make a notice board. At the top of each board, they pinned pieces of paper designating ownership. Kathy Farley wrote, "Kathy. Do not touch!" at the top of her board, and underneath she pinned the piece of paper shown in Figure 3.4.

When I asked Ellie what Kathy had meant by change (chage) the inside, she explained that one of Kathy's jobs was to change the furniture around. The following is a transcript of my conversation with Ellie (nine years and two months):

Denny:	"Ellie, water grass, clean house." That's "Ellie's Board" "Louise's Board." Who wrote that?
Ellie:	Louise.
Denny:	Louise wrote that one. Who wrote "Ellie's board"?
Ellie:	Me.
Denny:	And there's Kathy Farley: "Do not touch!" says Kathy Farley, and what has she written here? "My job, watering the grass and change the inside." What does she mean by that? "Change the inside"?
Ellie:	Change the furniture around.
Denny:	So the blackboard isn't up here anymore, right?

	And you have these here instead. And you have a book here.
Ellie:	That's my notebook from last year and I got a new one this year.
Denny:	So you brought this one up to the clubhouse.
Ellie:	We use it to write things in, and we have a desk.
Denny:	And you have a desk in here. And is there anything in that little note pad?
Ellie:	Um. Usually this is where I write down most of my lists to bring things.
Denny:	Is there anything in there now?
Ellie:	Well, there's Nan's picture.
Denny:	Nan drew that? She was here? (Nan was one year and eleven months of age.)
Ellie:	Yes. And there's a list.
Denny:	And what's this list for?
Ellie:	Oh, we were playing a game. We were playing restaurant, writing down all the things. Louise wanted breakfast.
Denny:	She was?
Ellie:	She was the guest.
Denny:	The guest and you were—?
Ellie:	I was the waitress.
Denny:	You were the waitress and was Kathy here too?
Ellie:	Kathy was at school I think. We had a day off from school.

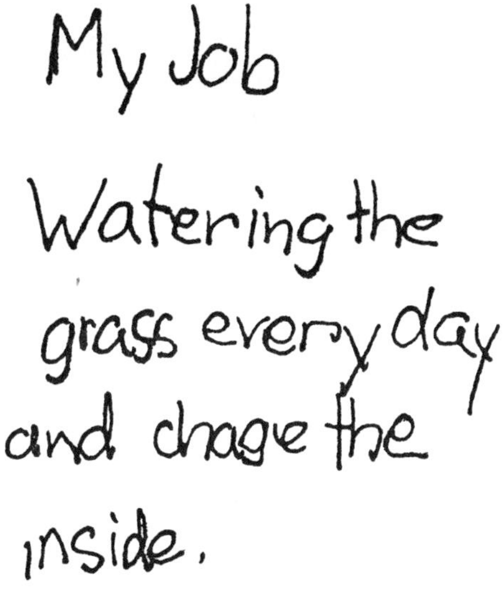

My Job

Watering the
grass every day
and change the
inside.

Fig. 3.4

Ellie, Kathy and Louise took their membership to the "tin shed" club very seriously. They each contributed items to furnish the clubhouse, and, as the notes imply, they spent much of their time organizing the interior decorations. On one occasion, Ellie and Kathy spent an entire afternoon in Kathy's house planning what they would need to furnish the shed. Karen Farley gave me the list they had made (see Figure 3.5).

The following spring the club members were once again planning their activities, and Ellie and Kathy began cleaning up the old tin shed after its winter abandonment. Kathy Farley recently formed another club with Bonnie King. Kathy was playing at Bonnie's house, and together they organized a club in which James was a member. Once again, print was used in many of the negotiations. Kathy and Bonnie designed membership forms which included the name, school, and birthdate of each member. Each member filled out the form and received a club pass on which his or her name was written. Kathy and Bonnie also wrote out the club rules (see Figure 3.6).

Exploring the Technological Environment through the Use of Print
In addition to learning ways of dealing with one another through the medium of print, the children are learning about organizing a business establishment, marketing products, conducting financial transactions, and using computer technology.

When Kathy and Debbie Farley turned their downstairs bathroom into a beauty salon, much of their time was spent organizing the establishment. Karen Farley commented afterwards that once they had worked it all out, they quickly lost interest in the game, adding that it seemed to her that it was the period of organization that the girls really enjoyed. Kathy made a sign which she taped to the bathroom door. It said, "Kathy Farley's Style Place." Opposite, on the child gate on the stairs, Kathy stuck another sign which read, "waiting room."

In a similar manner, Kathy and Louise planned to have a restaurant in Kathy's garage. They sat on the floor of the garage and wrote out menus (see Figure 3.7). The menus were identical. Later that day, I found the menus abandoned on the floor of the garage.

I asked Louise about the menus. She told me of their restaurant plans, explaining that they were going to have red-check tablecloths and that Kathy was going to take the money in the morning while she was the waitress, and in the afternoon, she was going to take the

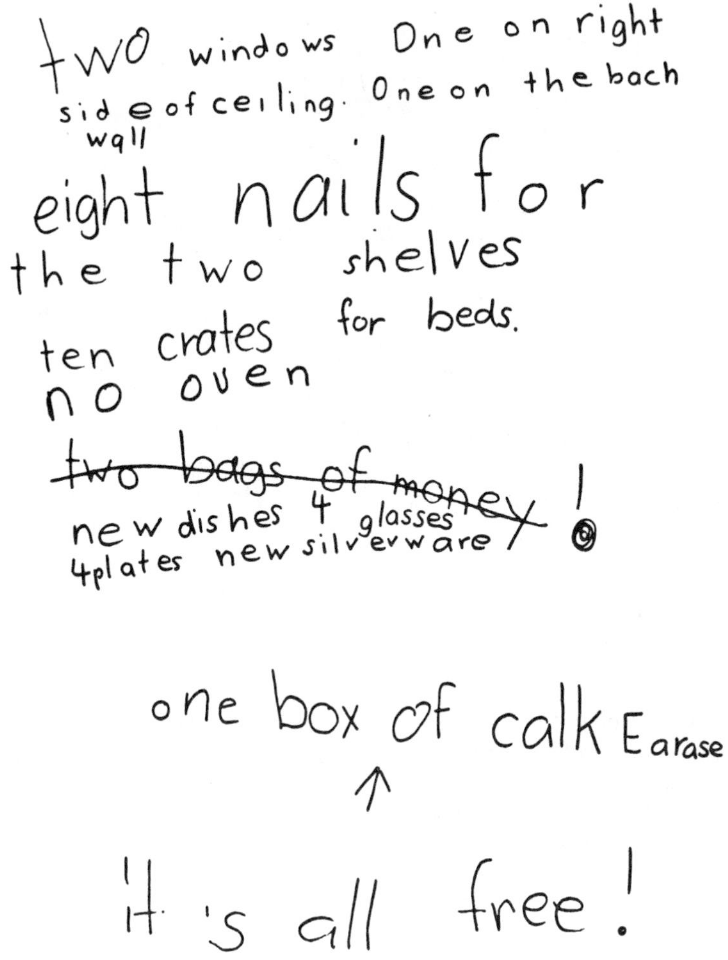

two windows One on right
side of ceiling. One on the back
wall

eight nails for
the two shelves

ten crates for beds.
no oven

~~two bags of money~~ |
new dishes 4 glasses
4 plates new silverware ⊙

one box of calk E arase
↑

It 's all free !

Fig. 3.5

money while Kathy was the waitress. I asked Louise who made the
first list; she replied, "nobody." "Then how did you write them?"
"Together," Louise explained. "Kathy would say something and
we'd both write it down. Then I'd say something and we'd write that
down."

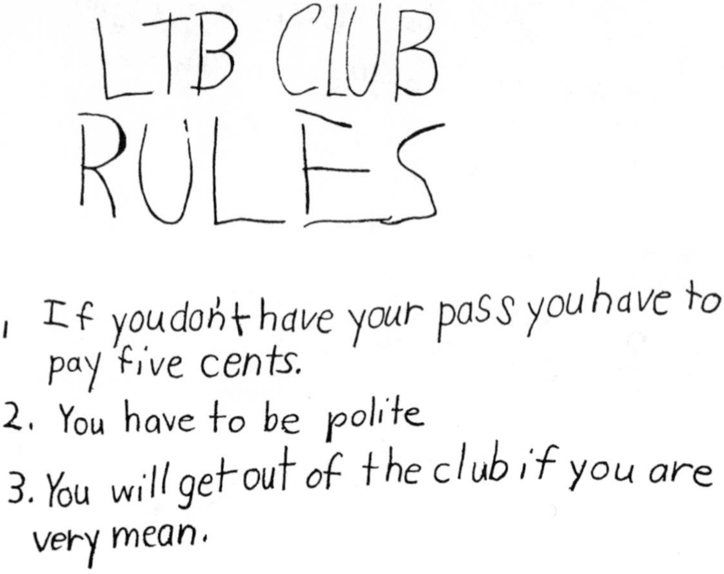

LTB CLUB RULES

1. If you don't have your pass you have to pay five cents.
2. You have to be polite
3. You will get out of the club if you are very mean.

Fig. 3.6

Many similar activities were noted as the study progressed, and the parents spoke of projects their children had planned and then lost interest in once the organization phase was completed. One such game held the attention of Kathy and her friends for several hours before, on the brink of success, it was abandoned. Kathy was playing with Ben (Taylor) in my driveway. It was a hot day, and Kathy decided to sell water to the people who passed by. She went home and came back with two pitchers of water which she set down on a log. Kathy wrote a sign and attached it to a nearby bush. She had written "cold water one dime." Louise (Taylor) joined Kathy and Ben. Kathy left them by the log with the water while she went to find some customers. A few minutes later, Kathy rushed back and announced that some children who lived along the street were coming to buy water. Not wanting to intrude, I retreated into the house. At lunch time, I asked Louise what had happened. Louise explained that the children had not wanted to pay a dime for a glass of water, and then she added that it was OK because they had fun with them anyway riding bicycles up and down the street. After lunch, Kathy and

Fig. 3.7

Debbie brought a card table from their house and placed it in a more prominent position on the grass near the edge of the road. Kathy made a new sign with a green pen. She wrote "Ice water! one dime each glass." Louise and Ben joined Kathy and Debbie, and a few minutes later, Ellie Dawson arrived. The five children played while they waited for customers. Debbie and Ben climbed a nearby tree while Kathy, Louise, and Ellie practiced headstands on the grass. Some time later, Kate, who was twelve, walked up the road and joined the group. Nobody had bought any water. Kate added "COLD" to the sign with a purple pen. Then she wrote "3 for 25" on the right side of the sign. Nobody bought any water. The children continued to play as they waited, tumbling on the grass and riding their bicycles up and down the street. Kate added to the sign, "VERY GOOD FOR YOU DOESN'T ROT TEETH LIKE LEMONADE" (see Figure 3.8). There were still no customers. Kate went home. She came back with a pitcher of lemonade. Kathy took down the sign and gave it to Kate who turned it over and wrote "ICE COLD LEMONADE," and underneath she wrote "10¢." Some adults walking along the street

Fig. 3.8

bought glasses of lemonade. As the third customer walked away, six children crowded around the lemonade stand giggling. They were changing the sign. Kathy was going over the price with the purple pen. Kate laughed and said, "We're lowering the price after we've served the customers!" Kathy changed the price to five cents (see Figure 3.9). A few minutes later, the children abandoned the lemonade stand, and Kathy tore down the sign. Later the stand was dismantled, and no more lemonade was sold that summer; once the organizational phase of the game was completed, the children lost interest in the enterprise—they had discovered how to market their product.

Fig. 3.9

In addition to group activities, many of the children's solitary pursuits included print as a means of utilizing the technological complexities of their social environment. The process of adopting a baby includes the use of computer technology as Sandy Lindell (eight years and seven months) pointed out in the game she played while waiting for some friends to arrive. Sandy decided to adopt a baby. On a small piece of paper from a spiral note pad, she wrote the necessary information.

Sandy L. Lindell

10.66   3 months

Anne Brown
Melissa L. Lindell

Sandy explained that this was an adoption paper; pointing to her name at the top of the page, she said she had signed the paper. Sandy continued by showing me the signature of Anne Brown, who was the director of the adoption agency. Pointing to the name at the bottom of the paper, she said that Melissa L. Lindell was the name of the baby that she was adopting. I asked Sandy what the "10.66" meant, and she replied that Melissa had cost ten dollars and sixty-six cents, and pointing to the other side of the paper, she added "at three months." Sandy then turned the paper over and showed me what she had written on the back (see Figure 3.10).

Fig. 3.10

Sandy explained that the information on the front of the paper was fed to the computer where it was checked out. The computer then printed out the findings "She is a good <u>mother</u>!!" Sandy had pushed the point of her pencil through the paper many times, simulating the key punch holes of a computer card.

This is an excellent example of a child engaging in a writing activity of which the parent is unaware. When I showed Laura Lindell the piece of paper which I had found in a corner of Sandy's room, she looked amused and said that she had not known about it. Laura went on to speak of a newspaper article about an adoption which had resulted in a court case. Laura had been discussing the case with Sarah and Beth. Sandy had been listening to their conversation and had asked them to explain the article.

While Sandy Lindell was using computer technology to adopt a baby, Kathy Farley (seven years and six months) devised a complex matrix to ensure equity in the sleeping arrangements of her dolls and teddy bears. Kathy discussed her sleeping chart, which we found under her bed while looking at the writing in her room.

Denny:	What's this? A sleeping chart? "Monday, Tuesday, Wednesday, Thursday, Friday, Saturday, Sunday."
Kathy:	I haven't been keeping it up.
Denny:	What do all these mean: "Mellow, Piggy, Tom"?
Kathy:	Those are my toys and Sunday only Daizy sleeps.
Denny:	Only Daizy sleeps. Friday Joy sleeps. But the others didn't? How does it work? You tell me.
Kathy:	You have to put a check down. Monday I have to sleep with Mellow and Daizy, Tuesday I have to sleep with Piggy and Daizy, Wednesday I have to sleep with Tom and Daizy, Thursday I have to sleep with Dorothy and Daizy, and Friday I have to sleep with Joy and Daizy, Saturday I have to sleep with Fuzzy and Daizy, and then on Sunday just Daizy.
Denny:	That's wonderful. Do you know who I'd like to meet?
Kathy:	Who?
Denny:	I'd like to meet Daizy.

CONCLUSIONS

Merleau-Ponty (1973) states that the clarity of language is before us "in what the infinitesimal gestures of any scrawling on the paper . . . reveals to the horizon as their meaning." My interpretation of literacy and the social organization of everyday life uses this notion to emphasize that print is one medium through which children are learning to master their surroundings.

Chukovsky (1968) speaks of the invention and construction of language by the preschool child, and Ferreiro (1978), speaking specifically of written language, writes of children reinventing language and making it their own. In both instances, the authors are speaking of the form of language. In this study children actively constructed the functions of literate language from a very young age. Goodman, Goodman, and Burke support the position that children learn to comprehend the purposes of print before they understand the alphabetic nature of written language; they write of children learning "to organize the print in their environment" (1978, p.15). I would rephrase their proposition and write that children learn to organize their environment through the use of print. The focus of their attention is not the print per se, but the social organization of their everyday lives. Print is one means of accomplishing this. Surrounded by the literate language activities of their parents, the children come to use print themselves, inventively constructing literate language uses in the mediation of their experiences of one another. McDermott writes, "People use words to make sense of each other, to encourage or hurt each other, to celebrate each other and to strike each other down" (1977, p. 167). All of these uses of language can be seen in the writings of the children. From a very young age, they are using print to salute and to hurt one another. From "I love you," "I hope you are feeling better," "You're fired from the club," to a simple birthday "Hello," the children are using print to mediate their experiences with family and friends.

While the children learn to use print in the mediation of their social relationships, the data also show that they are using print to explore the technological environment in which they live. Scribner and Cole write that "social organization creates the conditions for a variety of literate activities," and they go on to emphasize that "different types of text reflect different social practices" (1978a, p. 35). The data I have collected suggests that children learn of the multiplicity of literate activities as they learn of different social practices. Playing at restaurants includes writing menus as well as bills, while the adoption of a baby includes the computer screening of the prospective mother. Print in various forms is embedded in the social practices that the children explored.

4

Family Literacy and the Children's Emerging Awareness of Written Language

Absorbed in the present, the child during the first years of his life does not proceed on the basis of a conscious intention to retain material for future use. (Istomina, 1948, p. 15)

A word without meaning is an empty sound. (Vygotsky, 1962, p. 120)

The parents noted a shift marked by the inclusion of more specific learning experiences within the home as their children began to learn to read and write in school. Using references to this transitional phase as a point of entry into the data, I have attempted to follow the parents in their reconstruction of the children's early literacy experiences and to establish some possible relationships between the literate activities of the families and the children's emerging awareness of written language forms.

SOCIALLY EMBEDDED READING AND WRITING ACTIVITIES

In talking of their children's early reading and writing experiences, the parents often emphasized that they had not tried specifically to teach their children to read or write. Such statements were often followed by a wry smile and a tale of what had happened when they had tried to teach them. Donna King spoke of Bonnie before she went to school: "It seemed to me that she should be able to read, but if I tried to encourage her in any way it was just a big scene. She apparently wasn't really ready when I think of it." Similarly, Nina Simms spoke of Andrew who was then three years and nine months. She said:

> He's really not that terrific with colors, makes mistakes many times between yellows and greens, and I said, "My God, I've got to sit down with him and work with him," and when I try he doesn't want to be bothered, he doesn't want to.

Nina also spoke of Carol trying to teach Andrew the alphabet, but again Andrew was not interested. A year later, Nina told me that Andrew was writing his name, knew the alphabet, and was pretty good at recognizing colors. She ended up by saying, "What happened? He just seemed to put it together!" I cannot answer Nina's question, but the data do provide some interesting clues to what is undoubtedly an extraordinarily complex process.

Unnoticed Momentary Writing Activities

Many of the children's writing activities pass unnoticed as the children's momentary engagement merges with the procession of other interests. Nan Farley provided a wonderful example of such passing moments (see Figure 4.1). I visited Karen Farley to take photographs of the print in her home. Kathy and Debbie were at school while Nan (two years and two months) was "helping" Karen in the kitchen. After taking a number of photographs in the living room, I paused in front of a small table where a pencil was lying on a piece of paper. I snapped the shutter just before an unconcerned Nan (her father is an avid photographer) moved into the viewfinder. She picked up the pencil and began to "write." I quickly snapped the shutter and moved around and took a photo from another angle. Trying for a fourth shot, I shifted to a new frame, but Nan was gone—she moved out of the viewfinder and on to some new activity. It is possible to gauge the intensity of her interest from the photographs; otherwise it would have seemed nothing more than a passing gesture in an array of transitory moments. Although Karen had come into the room and had watched me taking the photographs, she did not remember the incident.

Karen's difficulty in recalling Nan writing is not unusual. Even when I showed the mothers the scraps of paper collected from their homes, they were often uncertain as to whom they belonged or, for that matter, when they had been produced. This is well illustrated by Jill Langdon's comments when we looked at some of the papers she found in a cupboard drawer in her living room. She hesitated several times before designating ownership and was often unsure if the papers were this year's or last year's writing endeavors. She found a drawing of a racing car which she said Ken had drawn. At that moment, Ken walked by and said, "I didn't draw that," and he told Jill that one of his friends had drawn it. Ken went off telling his mother he was going to draw one of his racing cars so that she would know what his looked like. Jill continued looking at the papers and

Fig. 4.1

Nan writing: Fleeting moments that fade unnoticed into other moments and other activities. I was so taken aback by the way that Nan passed through the view finder that I forgot to take the fourth photograph. To give some appreciation of the fleeting moment, I have used the initial photograph in the fourth position in the sequence.

stopped at two typed pages. She paused and said that she was not sure who had typed them. Reasoning aloud, she argued that she did not think Steven (four years and ten months) would have had the staying power to type so much, but that, on the other hand, Ken (seven years, nine months) would not have been content to type without writing something. Ken arrived back with a drawing of a car. After looking at it, Jill asked him who had typed the two pages. Ken replied, "Steven."

We finished looking at the papers, and I followed Jill into the kitchen where she was preparing a Chinese meal. She showed me a cookbook and told me of her Chinese cooking class. Moving around the kitchen while we talked, I picked up a piece of yellow lined paper off a counter top (see Figure 4.2). I asked Jill if it was for my collection. She looked at it and said, "No, I don't know where that came from." Steven walked into the kitchen and I asked him if he knew anything about the paper. He said, "Sure, I just did it." While we were talking, Steven was drawing letters. No one was watching him, and no one had seen him put the paper on the counter top—a perfect example of unnoticed momentary writing activities.

Fig. 4.2

The Reinvention of Writing Forms

Goody (1968) writes of the reinvention of written language forms when he speaks of the nonliterate adults he has known who have "taught themselves how to keep minimal records connected with their jobs" (p. 299). During the three years of the study, the children's active involvement in the reinvention of written language forms was documented. Once again, their engagement was often momentary and unnoticed, but there were some longer episodes where children sought the participation of a parent or sibling.

When Andrew was in his fourth year, he became noticeably interested in the alphabet. A set of plastic letters was kept in the television room. Andrew occasionally used them to form his name, but for the most part he had unconventional ways of playing with them. Nina spoke of his "making his own letters" by turning the plastic letters around to form new shapes. Nina described how Andrew used the **I** and the **C** to make **D**, and of his taking two **C** s to make **S**. She explained that he would make a new letter and then come up to her and ask, "What letter does that look like?" Nina would then join in the game. However, Nina laughed and added, "But if I suggest it he says, 'boring!!' "

James King (three years and eight months) constructed letters during one visit to my home. Donna was sitting with me at a table listening to a tape of the stories her family had recorded. James was on the floor playing with my son's wooden blocks. The blocks come in all shapes and sizes for building bridges, castles, and roads, but they can also be used to construct such things as letters. While Donna and I talked and listened to the tape, James played. After a while, he called out "*U!*" He had put two of the curved blocks together, and it did indeed look like a *U*. Donna turned around and said, "That's right, *U*." She joined James on the floor and started sorting through the blocks. After a few seconds, she said, "If we add some more we could make an *O*." She added some blocks to the *U* and said, "What's that?" James chirped "*O!*" Donna laughed and said, "a squared-off *O*." She tried to make a *W*, but it did not work. She then looked at the shape that James was making and said, "Here, what's that one? Does it look a little bit like a *Y*?" They laughed. James pointed to the letters: "This is *O*, that's a *Y*." Donna responded, "Right." James moved on and began to unpack a bag of cars and trucks, while Donna came back to the table and left him to play. We talked about James learning the alphabet. Donna commented that she was unsure of how many letters he knew. She spoke of him writing with chalk on the driveway and of the letters he had made with Bonnie, explaining that he had "made some like capital *H*, ones that have lots of nice straight lines." She then added, "But I don't know how many he can really do because we haven't worked. He recognizes most of the letters now, but I don't know how many he can write."

At the conclusion of the project, I talked with the parents about my perspectives of family literacy. Discussing the reinvention of written language forms with Donna King, I spoke of the morning James had used the blocks to make letters. Donna said that he probably made the letters because he was aware of my interest in reading and writing. I asked Donna if the activity was new, and she replied that it was not. James was making letters at home. We then talked of literacy displays—activities to demonstrate skills—and Donna agreed that this was such an occasion.

Ben (my son) used the same blocks in another display. One day he spent several hours building an edifice to mark the visit of the friend from whom he had borrowed the blocks. When the friend arrived, Ben took her to see his building. It was no more nor no less than his usual endeavors, but this time it was a block display for a friend who had a definite interest in his building.

The children's constructions were not limited to the reinvention of letters; their creation of words kept pace with their alphabetic inventions. A few weeks before James constructed the letters with the blocks, Donna said she wanted to show me the first word James had made. She took me into her kitchen, and there on the refrigerator door was the word AJAX. James had made the word and then asked Donna what it said. The only explanation Donna could give for his choice of a word was that when he visited the bathroom, he could see the Ajax container. Donna later said that James had started combining the magnetic letters into groups. He then asked her what each word said. Donna explained, "Sometimes we have to remove a letter or two or add one to make it say something."

Andrew Simms also made words. One Sunday, when he was four years and four months, Andrew visited my home with his family. While Andrew and Carol played with my children, Louise and Ben, Nina and Azar told us of their recent vacation. Nina showed me photographs they had taken. Under each photograph, Nina had written relevant information about the picture on tape designed for that purpose. Going through the photographs, we came to several on which Andrew had written. Nina laughed and pulled a face. She said that Andrew had wanted to write on the tape, but that she would not let him, so he had taken three of the photographs and gone to find some Scotch tape. Andrew cut the tape in strips and stuck one piece on the bottom of each photograph. Then he wrote under each picture. These resembled:

QILTA, AITOD, Q+A
OQO

In the past year, Andrew has become increasingly interested in writing. He writes his name on his drawings and writes messages to his family. On Valentine's Day, when he was four years and ten months, he drew a picture of smiling people, decorated it with hearts, and with Carol's assistance, wrote "Happy Valentine's I love you." At about the same time, Andrew asked Carol to write the numbers from one to ten on a piece of paper; he copied the numbers underneath. He then asked her to write, "To the whole family from Andrew," and once again he copied the message. When Nina showed me this example of Andrew's writing, she noted that it was a new enterprise and that Andrew was continually asking them to write messages he dictated.

Name writing was a notable feature of the children's literate endeavors. Hildreth (1936) states, "Name writing results from the child's interest in practicing, not solely from the child's being told how to do it" (p. 301). When Debbie Farley was about the same age as Andrew she too became increasingly interested in writing. She wrote her name on odd scraps of paper, and she began writing her name on the many pictures she drew. Once she used her name as a border for the picture that she had drawn:

```
DEBBIE

D       D.

E       E

B       B

B       B

I       I

EDEBBIE
```

Another time her name was the picture:

```
E   E   E   E

I   I   I   I

B   B   B   B

B   B   B   B

E   E   E   E

D   D   D   D
```

During this year Debbie began writing messages such as "DEAR-MOMDEBBIE I AM SENDING A CARD." In addition to writing messages, she became increasingly interested in practicing how to write. During one of my visits, Karen and I found a piece of paper on Debbie's (four years and ten months) desk (see Figure 4.3). We puzzled over the paper for some time. The first line was easy to make out, "The chick and t." Karen said she thought it should say, "The Chick and the Duck" as she was sure Debbie was copying the title of a book they had read recently. We could not find the book. We then worked out that the second line was probably the dedication, "To Libby," and the third line was the beginning of the text, "A duck."

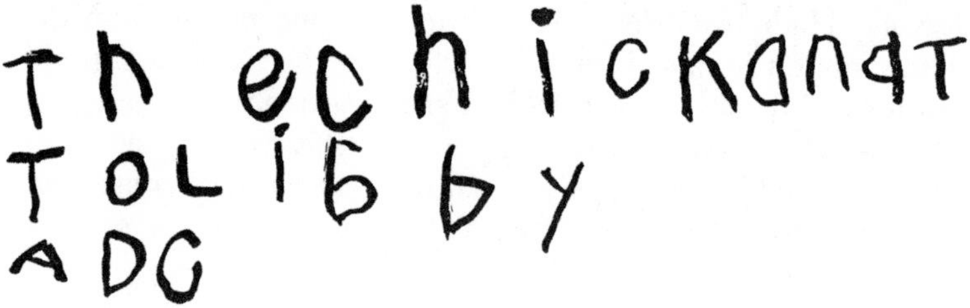

Fig. 4.3

Debbie's heightened involvement in writing came at approximately the same time as the increased interest of Andrew and Steven, when all three children were in their final year of nursery school. Kindergarten would be the next step. The parents had referred to this development during the initial stages of the study as they spoke of their older children's increasing involvement with written language during their kindergarten years. A more detailed analysis of the school-related nature of Debbie's, Andrew's, and Steven's deepening interest in language will be presented later in this chapter.

LEARNING TO "READ": SYMBOLS, SIGNS, AND STORIES

Szwed (1977) speaks of reading signs as a public event involving a different set of skills than private reading. In this study reading signs is a public event shared by parents and children. We can only guess what it is the child reads. Lee Farley spoke of pointing out pedestrian signals to Kathy. He explained, "Walk, don't walk, these are biggies when you look at signs a lot. Yeh, walk is green and don't walk it flashes and is in red." Lee went on to emphasize how many signs in the city are easy for the young child to recognize because they are logos.

The parents introduced each child to the pragmatic signs and symbols that are deeply embedded in the social situation and nearly always functional. If you want to cross a busy street, you wait until the pedestrian signal says "Walk." You do not cross when it flashes "Don't Walk." However, the children's introduction to extended written language forms was less businesslike, because it occurred for the most part when they listened to the stories read by their parents.

Learning to "Read" Symbols and Signs

One of the first signs Ken Langdon learned to "read" was "TWO GUYS." Jill said he had known the sign since he was quite small, for he would help her find it as they sped along the highway looking for the store. Jill explained that once Ken knew the sign, he would point to it whenever they passed the store, and she added that Steven had then learned to "read" the sign by taking his cues from Ken.

Sometimes the words that the children learned to "read" were words that they were learning to say. Karen Farley spoke of Kathy learning to "read" signs as she learned to talk, and she spoke of remembering that when Kathy was in a backpack, she would point to the signs that Karen and Lee had taught her. Karen used as an example "EXIT," which she described as one of Kathy's first words. Lee also spoke of Kathy's early experiences with print, explaining:

> We pointed them out and worked with them that way. I guess no attempt at really reading them just "catch that word". . . She was in the backpack then, we were in New York. That started that routine, of recognizing "that says pizza," and so as you walk along you point out words. You can point them out all over the place.

When pointing out the pizza sign, Karen and Lee would sometimes stop and buy slices of pizza. Kathy would chew a crust from the pizza as she bobbed along in the backpack. Ken Langdon learned that once they spotted the sign of "TWO GUYS," they would leave the highway and visit the store. James King knew that cars were supposed to stop at a red light, for as Joe King commented of James a few months before his third birthday, "One time I went through and I missed, I think I started too soon or something and he said, 'Police, police is going to come.'" The signs and symbols that the children have learned to recognize are more than empty sounds, for they have a function in their environment. The words that the parents point out have no intrinsic merit, simply a practicality in daily life.

While learning signs (including MacDonalds) when out with their parents, the children also learned of the print in their homes. As the ways the children used print increased, the forms of written language to which they became accustomed grew more complex. Thus Debbie wrote a birthday "Hello" when she was three years and six months, and some eighteen months later, she wrote to her mother "DEARMOMDEBBIE I AM SENDING A CARD."

The parents often spoke of the difficulties of finding well-defined examples of the times when their children came into contact with print. However, over the years, many references have been made to situations where "reading" played a part. Leo Langdon's comments are typical. After acknowledging that "a lot of things go on that you're not aware of," he gave many useful examples of situations that occurred when Ken was in first grade. He spoke of the games they played with Ken and Steven and of what happened when they introduced a new game. He explained, "We would read the instructions to them. We would ask them and they would know where the instructions were, that they were on the inside of the box or whatever." Leo went on to talk of the words appearing in the coloring books that Ken and Steven enjoyed, and of the stickers which came with some of the toys and models that Ken made. Speaking of Ken, Leo explained:

> He loves to put stickers on things and on his models and that. He just put together a couple of planes, I think, and he took the stickers and wanted to know what the stickers said, he would pick out where they went on the diagram and he could put them on the model.

Leo also spoke of the reading he shared with Ken, explaining that occasionally he read newspaper articles to him, but more often they shared the articles in Ken's *Ranger Rick*. Talking of watching television, Leo said, "He'll say, 'What's on now?' and I'll look it up and tell him what's on, and he'll put it on the station he wants."

The question of television's influence came up many times in my conversations with the parents, and I have often visited their homes when the children have been watching it. Sometimes the mothers turned the television on as I arrived so the children could watch as we talked. Usually the children watched cartoons. Most of the parents spoke of "Sesame Street" as an influential program in the lives of their children, especially with regard to learning to say the alphabet. Barry Lindell said that by watching "Sesame Street" while they were very young, his children learned to say the alphabet long before they knew what it was. Only Donna and Joe King were critical of this program. Donna explained that neither of her children were particularly fond of "Sesame Street," and she blamed the frenetic pace of the program for their lack of interest.

In considering the influence of "Sesame Street" and television in general, it is important to note how siblings influence each other's viewing habits. The parents often noted that their younger children were not the "Sesame Street" fans that their older siblings had been. The parents of the four families with preschool children also spoke of their younger children learning the alphabet later than their first borns. Indeed, from the parents' many comments and my observations, such programs as "Sesame Street" and "The Electric Company" are far more influential in the lives of the first borns, for by the time the second child has come along, the first one has discovered the delights of Woody Woodpecker. Lee Farley gave a neat description of the situation. He explained:

> I'm a big "Sesame Street" freak because I think kids that watch that learn something. I'm not sure what. But I think that's helped Kathy. I know Debbie is not watching as much of it as Kathy did because Kathy wants to watch something else, and once Debbie catches on that whatever the cartoon is might be a little more interesting than "Sesame Street," or big sister is doing it and therefore I want to do the same, "Sesame Street" goes downhill.

At the present time, I can offer few insights into the degree to which television helps or hinders the children's learning to "read" signs and symbols. Clearly, the "Sesame Street" Alphabet Song is one that the preschool children knew, and often, as with the Lindell children, they can sing the song long before they associate it with the written alphabet. One wonders if the song is always learned by watching television, for, as Nina Simms pointed out, Andrew learned the song at nursery school and not from "Sesame Street." What

Andrew and the other children learned of the many words embedded in the cartoons they watch remains a mystery.

Fortunately, the children's awareness of printed forms was easier to tap in situations when they were not watching television programs, and I often observed them at such times. Two occasions have long impressed me. Once I visited Karen Farley to see if I could do any shopping for her as she was housebound with a feverish Nan. Karen was putting Nan and Debbie to bed for their afternoon naps when I arrived, so we talked for a few minutes on the doorstep. Karen said that Nan was much better, and the conversation turned to the summer sales which were taking place in the local shops. Debbie (four years and eight months) interrupted this discussion by holding up a piece of paper for me to read. Frowning at me, she said, "Denny remember." On the paper was the reminder, "Nan and Debbie are sleeping. Please be quiet." It was the note Karen usually taped to the front door when the girls took their naps. Although Debbie was not reading in the conventional way, she knew the meaning of the writing and used it effectively to tell me to go. The note has recently been shortened to "napping."

On another occasion when I was reading some stories to Steven Langdon (three years and ten months), I asked Steven if he could show me some of the words in his room. Steven examined several of his toys, found some words, and showed them to me. He knew where to find the words; he picked up a truck and held it up for me to see without actually looking at the words himself. When I talked with Leo Langdon of the words on the toys that the boys played with, he said he was really unsure of whether they were aware of them or not.

During one of my visits to the Simms's home, Andrew showed me the books in his room, and I read several stories to him. Then Andrew "read" to me one of the "Clifford" stories. We sat on the floor, and Andrew turned over the pages showing me the pictures while "reading" the tale. At the end of the story, Clifford puts out a fire. Andrew explained, "The fire was inside the house so he ran out just in time. And he take off the fire. Splosh at the window. And he was a hero." I asked Andrew how he knew that Clifford was a hero. He replied, "Right here he is." Andrew pointed to the medal which hung around Clifford's neck in the last picture of the story. On the medal was written "HERO."

Learning to "Read" Stories

In the early stages of the research, the parents often called my attention to the importance they attached to the stories they shared with their children. In every instance they stressed that they had not read to their children to specifically teach them to read, but they did acknowledge that listening to stories was important. To find out more about such story-sharing occasions, special methods of data collection were devised, and a detailed study was made of the social context of story reading (Taylor, 1980).

Story sharing was intricately woven into the social processes of family life, with a broad panoply of purposes, facilitating communication between parents and children and forming one medium for the development of a shared social heritage. In addition, story sharing developed into a routine which was highly dependent upon the individual educative styles of the participants. It was an occasion with a cumulative context, and one in which distinctly original family agendas evolved. More important, reading and telling stories and talking about the pictures and texts were initially woven together as the parents endeavored to impart to the child the appropriate stategies and procedures necessary for the story to ultimately make sense. In this atmosphere the children experimented with "reading" the text.

As Nan Farley demonstrated, such experimentation can begin at a very young age. I visited the Farley home when Nan was one year and eleven months of age. Karen asked Nan to get me a book from her room. Nan toddled off, but came back empty-handed, so Karen went with her to find a book. Before Nan was born, her bedroom had been Kathy's and Debbie's playroom, and their books as well as many Fisher Price toys still lined the shelves on one wall of the room. One by one, Nan took down the books from the shelves and showed me the covers before replacing them. Karen took three "Golden Books" and handed them to Nan. Nan promptly plopped down. She put two of the books on the floor and opened the third to one of the middle pages. Without any words, she "read" the story, rhythmically making the sounds of reading, and then stopping every few seconds to turn the book for me to see the pictures. Karen left the room, and Nan, noticing that her mother had gone, tucked the book she was "reading" under her arm and, after making sure that I had the other books, quickly followed her mother.

Karen was in the living room. Nan got up on the couch and continued looking at the book. No longer "reading," she contented herself by looking at the pictures and turning the pages. She opened the book at the title page and then examined the advertisement for Disney books on the back cover. Then she turned to the first page of the story and pointed at the puppies in the picture and said "puppy." During this visit to the Farley home, Karen and I talked of the words that Nan was learning to say as she looked at the picture books. Karen commented that when Nan looked at the pictures, she was often introduced to new objects and new words.

I asked Karen if Nan listened to the bedtime stories with Kathy and Debbie, and she said that Nan was a very active participant. Karen explained, "She's very vocal and gets right in there." In listening to the audio recordings of the Farley family reading, there is a noticeable change in the way that the stories were shared pre- and post-Nan. In the early recordings, there was very little preparation for reading and many long stretches on the tape of Karen reading. In the later tape, Nan had joined the group, and much of Karen's time was spent in bringing Nan to the story and then trying to keep her there. At this time Kathy stopped listening to the bedtime stories.

Nan's activity and Karen's effort provide a vivid illustration of the early years of story sharing, for all of the parents spoke of this time as chaotic. Nina Simms provided the following description:

> But, of course, even though they'd want to hear it they wouldn't sit still to listen to it. So it was "let me finish this first," "come on let's, let's listen to the story" . . . there was a lot of action going on trying to finish the story. Now they will sit and listen to the whole thing. But at that time they would not.

Much of the parents' story reading time during these early years was spent completing the story. Parents spoke of paraphrasing the text and talking about the pictures as they introduced each child to the art of reading stories. While the children learned about the sounds of written language, they also learned the mechanics of reading a book. Where you start and which page you read next are all part of the story reading occasion. Thus when James King (two years and eight months) turned over a clump of pages, Donna quickly countered the move by saying, "Wait a minute; we missed some pages. Let's see, let's go back to where we were. Where were we? We're back here." And then, once the page was found, Donna gave a quick review of the text, "We saw all the bears," and then began reading, "Gloria, Emma, Anna, Johanna, and Hannah. They all lived in hollow trees." Donna was imparting to James that there was a logical order to the story that they must follow if the story is to ultimately make sense.

Like Nan Farley, James was also experimenting with reading the text while learning from his parents the appropriate strategies for turning pages. James also "read" stories and enjoyed playing with the text when reading with his mom and dad. Joe and James shared the joke of a "duggle bus" in a book about automobiles. They laughed when they reached the part about the duggle bus because they both knew it was really a double decker bus. James also played with his mother when he looked for the mouse in the picture of *Good Night Moon* by Margaret Wize Brown. Hidden in the game were the words of the text, and James would sometimes bring his mother back to the story by "reading" the next line on a page. The following is a section from the verbatim transcription:

James:	Where? Where Mom?
Donna:	Do you want me to give you a hint?
James:	(Points to mouse.)
Donna:	You've found him. (Laughs.)
James:	(Laughs.) Goodnight <u>Goodnight kittens.</u>*
Donna:	"Goodnight kittens."
James:	<u>Goodnight mittens.</u>
Donna:	"Goodnight."
James:	Where's mouse now? I don't know. Where Mom?
Donna:	Shall I give you a hint?
James:	Yeh.
Donna:	It's over somewhere on this page.
James:	Where?
Donna:	He climbed up on top of something.
James:	What?
Donna:	Well, look carefully. He's not on this side. Look on this page.
James:	Sss. (Laughs, points to the mouse.)
Denny:	There he is. (Laughs.)
Donna:	(Laughs.)
Denny:	He really is a tricky mouse.
Donna:	Yeh.
James:	<u>Goodnight</u> (little) <u>house.</u>**
Donna:	"Goodnight little house."
James:	<u>Goodnight mouse.</u>
Donna:	"(And) goodnight mouse."
James:	Where is mouse now? Give me a hint.

*Underlining indicates that James was using the words of the text.
**"Little" appears in the text, but was not said.

Such playing was often noted by the parents. Laura Lindell spoke of Barry "playing the buffoon," and Jill Langdon of Leo "hamming it up." From the many comments that parents made, it would seem that the stories with which they played were stories that the children knew well. Lee Farley made this point when he asked me if I had ever "read stories silly." He explained:

You change the words around. You pick a story they're familiar
with and, you know, "It was the night before Christmas and all
through the house the elephants were tramping." And they
howl. They think this is absolutely great. And you know, "I ran
to the window, threw up the sash and fell out." They think this is
absolutely ridiculous.

Lee went on to explain that the girls sometimes asked him to "read
silly," while at other times, they would say, "Read it right this time."
He added, "I don't know where I picked that up from. I just made it
up. I got tired of reading the same story."

The parents often spoke with dismay of the number of times their
children wanted to hear favorite stories. Jill Langdon talked of Steven
during his fourth year: "He will go through stages where he will pick
out a certain book and will read it for a couple of weeks." She spoke of
reading *The Little Engine that Could* for three weeks. Repetition is a
very important part of learning to read stories, for it is the stories they
have heard many times that the young children "read." Nina Simms
spoke of Andrew (three years and eight months) "reading," and she
explained:

He'll sit down and open the pages and pretend he's reading the
words. He's not reading the words but he sees the pictures and
he'll go along and tell the story. He'll do it by himself when I'm
not around. He'll sit in his own room on the floor and he'll take
out a book and say, "and the fish flips on the thing and the
motorcycle, oh, it went in the water," and he's telling the story
himself. He's reading out loud.

The story of the fish that flips was one of Andrew's favorite books,
and he had heard the story many times.

The children are also learning of reading as an interactive process,
for the parents spent much of their story-reading time relating events
in the stories to the everyday lives of their children. Donna King
spoke of making associations with the story, while Jill Langdon spoke
of the many experiences that they shared through books. At the
conclusion of one recorded story in which a small boy and an elephant
were lost, Nina Simms commented to Andrew, "See how people can
get lost like the little elephant when they don't stay near their mom-
mies? Right?" Andrew's immediate reply was, "Like I did." "Right,"
said Nina. "You remember that." Later, when Nina listened to the
recording, she spoke of Andrew getting lost at a shopping mall and of
her memories of her parents' distress when she had gone for walks on
her own as a very small child. The story provided Nina with the
opportunity of sharing with Andrew the social expectation that chil-

dren should stay close to their mothers, and those who do, do not get lost. Nina commented, "The kid doesn't stop to think of these things, he thinks he's just off exploring . . . of course, he doesn't think that mommy's walking over there, thinking he's behind." She added, "It clicked here, 'Like I did,' you see, it clicked that he got lost and he remembered."

As the reading of stories becomes intricately woven into the social processes of family life, the children learn to play with the text. From their preliminary ventures with the sounds of written language to their tentative forays with the words of the text, they learn of reading as an all-inclusive process. "Reading the pictures," "seeing what the page says," and "telling the story" are how the parents spoke of such occasions. Within this context the children began to navigate the pages in their interactions with the text.

THE INTRODUCTION OF SPECIFIC
SCHOOL-RELATED READING AND WRITING ACTIVITIES

There is a noticeable shift when the children start to learn to read and write in school. Reading and writing are lifted out of context and become the specific focus of attention. The children's new interest in print is integrated with their earlier experiences of written language. Throughout the transitional period, the activities that engage the children remain socially significant to their everyday lives.

School-Related Literate Activities

When Debbie Farley was four years and two months, her nursery school teacher told her mother that Debbie was becoming increasingly interested in numbers. Karen Farley said the teacher told her that Debbie was "crazy about them." On a dismal February afternoon, while Kathy played with Louise and Ben, Debbie and her mother went on a special outing to buy a book to help her draw numbers. Debbie was asked if she would like to stay and play, but the outing to buy the number book was more important to her and she did not hesitate to go with her mother. Later that afternoon, when Karen came to get Kathy, Debbie was with her. She was clutching a book. In it were numbers and letters drawn on specially lined paper. I asked Debbie who had chosen the book. She explained that she had told her mom that she wanted a book in which to practice writing numbers and letters, and that her mom had found it for her. There was a lot of talk in the following days about the book, and then nothing was said about it for a long time. Some eight months later, during a visit to the

Farley home, I asked Karen about the book, and she said that Debbie had got into the habit of writing in it just before her afternoon nap. Karen explained that just before she went to sleep, Debbie would spend a short time at her desk, and Karen noted that Debbie spoke of "doing her homework." Karen took me up to Debbie's room, and she showed me the book, and then, flipping the pages back and forth, she commented on the improvement in the way Debbie was forming both numbers and letters.

Debbie's interest in numbers and letters was not an isolated event. At this time Ellie Dawson helped Debbie to write the word "daddy." When Ellie let me see the inside of her clubhouse, I found some of Debbie's writing.

Denny: Do you have any other writing here? What's in here; can I look? (Looking in trash can.)

Ellie: Sure. Debbie was showing me how she can write daddy.

Denny: Who wrote this (pointing to "daddy" written on the paper)? (See Figure 4.4.)

Ellie: I wrote that one. And Debbie wrote that one. (See Figure 4.5.)

Denny: What happened? She sat down with you?

Ellie: Yes, she told me she had learned to write daddy in school the other day. She showed me how she could do it.

Denny: That's wonderful. Did you write this or did she write this first?

Ellie: She wrote that first and I said it should be a little bit smaller and I showed her the way that you stay on the lines and that it's the same size.

Fig. 4.4

Fig.4.5

The intricacies of events do not stop here; Debbie also became interested in words, and her specific interest seems school-related. During one trip to school Debbie also told me about her word box. Usually Debbie romped at the back of the car, but on that day, she sat at the front to tell me of her box. I asked her what words she had in the box, and she said, "popcorn, house, and wood." Later, Karen Farley explained that Debbie had brought a letter home from school asking them to buy her a word box. They had done this, and Debbie had taken it to school. Since then, Debbie had been asking for words. Debbie said what word she wanted, and Karen wrote it down. When Debbie had about ten words, she would ask Karen to help her say them. Another facet of this new interest in words was evident during the evening story-sharing occasion, for Karen commented that Kathy was often irritated when they read together because Karen had started pointing out some of the words to Debbie when Kathy just wanted to listen to the story. Debbie's preoccupation with words decreased over the following weeks as her teachers would not let her bring home the word box to which she attached so much importance.

Debbie's enthusiasm was short-lived and is reminiscent of the picture presented by Laura Lindell of her children's early and temporary interest in word games. Debbie's experiences do not seem to be in any way unusual. The children's interests were often short and intense; the parents picked up on their absorption, providing help and materials as they were needed. Clearly, however short-lived, the experiences changed things; Karen is still pointing out words to Debbie when she reads to her, and Debbie continues to write. Just the word box game was abandoned.

The Relevance of the Activities to the Lives of the Children

As new experiences are added to the family's agenda, old experiences fall into place. The temporal integration of literate experiences seems to set its own pace, and as Donna King so aptly put it, "I guess part of it is that you just don't know what goes into things until you see a kid learn them." Donna spoke of the work Bonnie had brought home from school during her kindergarten year and noted that she was surprised to find that many of the skills she was being taught were skills they had played with at home in the preceding years. She gave the example of rhyming words, noting that in some stories this was a feature they had played with, as Bonnie had loved the sounds and enjoyed the repetition.

In exploring this facet of family literacy, the question that constantly arose was the degree to which school-related activities are initiated by the child or by the parent. It seems that the children's heightened sensitivity to written language is in some ways balanced by the parents' response to this increasing awareness, and by their knowledge of the academic expectations imposed by society on the first-grade child. The following examples hint at the complexities of these interrelationships.

Andrew Simms was four years of age when he became increasingly interested in writing. He would dictate messages to members of his family, and then he would copy them. The messages that Andrew wrote never seemed to be divorced from the social situation in which they were written. The salutation that Andrew wrote to his family on Valentine's Day is an excellent example of his context-dependent writing. As Andrew's fifth year approached, he told his mother that he wanted to learn to read. His mother responded to the situation. Nina had been given a series of cards called "Form a Sound." On each card was a letter and a picture of a mouth forming the appropriate shape for forming the letter sound. Underneath was a word beginning with the appropriate sound and a picture of the object. Thus, on one of the cards was the letter *O* and a picture of a mouth shaped to make the *O* sound. Underneath was the word "over" and a picture of some sheep going over a fence. A school teacher had given Nina the cards to use with Andrew. This Nina attempted to do—with disastrous results. Andrew refused to cooperate, resisting any attempts that Nina made to work with him. Instead, he found his own uses for the cards. When the family bought new dining room furniture, he drew a picture on the back of a card; when the Winter Olympics were being televised, he used another card to make an American flag; and when Valentine's Day arrived, Andrew drew a picture of his family and wrote "Happy Valentine's I love you" on it. Best of all was the four-foot eagle he constructed by stapling many of the cards together. Nina spoke of the many hours Andrew spent cutting, stapling, and drawing before the eagle was finally completed. A few days after Andrew had constructed the eagle, Nina let me borrow it to use in a paper presentation. However, Nina telephoned when Andrew returned from nursery school to say that he was very upset with her for giving me the eagle. I returned it immediately. Some four months later, it was still hanging on their dining room wall, and Andrew was still very proud of his endeavor.

Nina is pursuing more school-related activities with Andrew. Andrew keeps telling her that he wants to read, and Nina, responding to his enthusiasm, is pointing out words in books. She asks him what letter individual words begin with, and Andrew sings his way through the "Sesame Street" Alphabet Song until he reaches the letter.

The experiences of Nina and Andrew are in no way uncommon. School-related activities are resisted if they are not socially significant to the child, but meaningful school-related reading activities can often find their place in the home. At the end of Ken Langdon's first-grade year, Jill voiced her concern that he might lose his momentum during the long summer months, and she said that she was going to encourage him to keep a journal. Toward the end of August, Jill brought the boys to lunch, and I asked her about Ken's journal. She said that it had not worked, explaining that between the daily events at the local park and their vacation, there just did not seem to be enough time. Later, Jill showed me what Ken had written (see Figure 4.6). The journal lasted four days.

In the fall of Ken's second-grade year, Leo Langdon went to Washington and bought a book about the presidents of the United States for Ken. Ken l♭ed the book. He traced the signatures of forty-three presidents. Ken became increasingly interested in writing

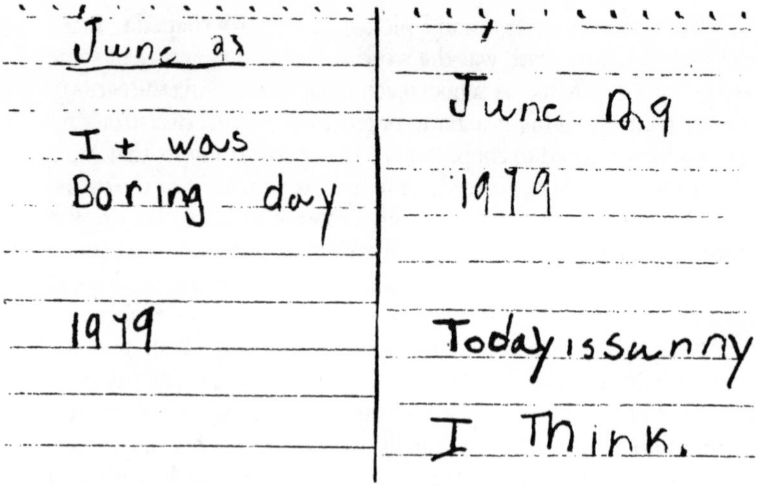

June 2?

I + was
Boring day

1979

June 29
1979

Today is sunny

I Think.

Fig. 4.6

in script, and he spent a lot of time writing his name and the names of the members of his family. Jill helped him with his writing and showed him how to write his spelling words in script.

CONCLUSIONS

Istomina's (1948) belief that, "Absorbed in the present, the child during the first years of his life does not proceed on the basis of a conscious intention to retain material for future use" is supported in this interpretation of family literacy, for the children of this study learned of print through the socially significant literate activities in which they engaged, and it was within this context that their awareness of written language forms developed. It was a whole language process in which listening, talking, reading, and writing grew as interrelated forms of a communicative system. While learning to talk, the children learned of the social significance of such signs as "Two Guys" and "exit," played with the reinvention of letters and words, and experimented with "reading" stories. There were no "empty sounds" (Vygotsky, 1962, p. 120), for the meanings of their words had immediate relevance to their everyday lives.

There does come a time when print per se becomes of intense interest to children. As long ago as 1936, Hildreth wrote of children's increasing practice of writing through the preschool years, and she notes that "as they mature they demand more help from their elders in achieving skill in writing." The children's increasing fascination with both writing and reading was well evidenced in the present research, and their fascination with print seems to occur when they have become highly sophisticated in their knowledge of the functional utility of print. Vygotsky writes, "Every function of the child's cultural development appears twice: first on the social level, and later, on the individual level . . . All the higher functions originate as actual relations between human individuals" (1978, p. 57). For these children, literacy evolved as an interpersonal process of functional utility, but with the advent of school and the social expectation of learning to read, literacy also became an intrapersonal process. Developing metalinguistic awareness (Ehri, 1978) of written language forms was added to the literacy agenda of the children. But still, the activities were meaningful in their everyday lives. They never lost the interpersonal characteristics; rather intrapersonal characteristics added another dimension to literate endeavors. Keeping a journal because a mother wishes her child to maintain momentum could not compare with learning script to be able to sign one's name like the presidents of the United States.

5

Family Literacy
in a Cultural Context

Modern education includes a heavy emphasis upon the functions of education to create discontinuities—to turn the child of the peasant into a clerk, of the farmer into a lawyer, the Italian immigrant into an American, and the illiterate into the literate. (Mead, 1943, p. 627)

This chapter considers literacy in a broader context. By juxtaposing the experiences of the families in this study with perspectives of family literacy gained from other sources, I support the view that literacy develops best in relational contexts which are meaningful to the young child.

Speaking of the Vai, a traditional society on the northwest coast of Liberia, Scribner and Cole (1978b) state, "Their writing and reading are not activities separate from their daily pursuits." Similarly for the families participating in this research, reading and writing are cultural activities intrinsic to their experiences. Consequently, reading and writing are introduced to the children as essential features of their language. Reading and writing join with speaking and listening in an elaboration of the families' existing associations.

TALKING AND LISTENING, READING AND WRITING

The parents often spoke of the importance of talking and listening to their children when they are learning to read and write. Azar Simms talked of listening to Carol and Andrew even though he was often tired when he came home from work, and he spoke with approval of the way Nina talked to the children "all the time." Nina emphasized the importance of talking with the children rather than at them, and she spoke of listening to them, commenting that so many parents do not listen to their children. Laura Lindell also emphasized the importance of listening and talking, commenting, "We talked about things all the time. I cannot believe that some of the kids I work with in kindergarten cannot communicate. Nobody talks to them." (When Sandy was in kindergarten Laura spent one afternoon a week in the classroom helping the children to write stories.)

The parents, however, never spoke directly of the ways these modes of communication came together, but they did offer some clues. One of the most intriguing aspects of our initial conversations was the way parents spoke of individual children reading, when it was understood that in the traditional sense of the word the children were most certainly nonreaders. Lee Farley stated "Kathy will read to Debbie or they'll read together. I can hear them up there for an hour at a time, sometimes when they should be asleep. But what the hell, if they're sitting quietly reading I don't care." At the time of this conversation, Kathy had just learned to read; however, Debbie was three and a half years of age and was most certainly a nonreader. Joe King spoke in a similar fashion about Bonnie when she was a baby. He noted, "She read, she seemed to read from the time she was very young. I think she would listen to stories from the time she was eight or nine months. She loved to listen."

The parents used the word "reading" in a similar way when sharing stories with their children. They talked to their children about reading beginning at a very early age. Typical comments were Jill Langdon asking Steven when he was three years of age, "Do you want to read to me today?" or Donna King asking two-year-old James, "Do you want to read about the summertime or wintertime?" Very often, reading and talking were linked by the parents, as with Nina Simms who said to Andrew when he was four years of age, "*Read* the story. OK tell me what it's all about." "Seeing what the page says" and "reading the pictures" were other variations. Just as many parents hold conversations with their babies, these parents read with their children; and just as they expected their children to talk, they expected them to read.

But what if one of the children failed? I put this question to each of the parents, and their comments implied that growing up illiterate was unthinkable. Lee Farley replied quickly to the question, stating firmly, "That's not an option. They'd learn to read. Learn to fend for themselves." Laura Lindell said she could not imagine that happening unless there was some kind of brain damage, a viewpoint held by most of the parents. Only Nina Simms said it would not be a matter of some brain dysfunction. Speaking specifically of Andrew, Nina emphasized how upset she would be if he did not learn to read. She explained, "Not that he wouldn't be intelligent enough, but that he wouldn't be interested enough." Nina added, "My God what can you do if you can't read!" and she conluded with a smile that she had also worried about Carol, but she had learned without any difficulty.

What would happen if one of the children actually failed? Fortunately, this has not happened, but the following incident does provide some insights. Sandy Lindell is the third child in a family of avid readers, but Sandy is not so inclined. Barry explained when she was in first grade, "Sandy is not as interested. I don't think that she is going to be the reader that the other two girls are. She will rarely pick a book out and sit and read it." During the three years of the study, no one has questioned Sandy's reading ability, for while it is well known among family and friends that she does not read as much as her sisters, it is equally well known that she is a good reader who simply prefers to listen to stories. When Sandy was about to enter fourth grade, she was still listening to stories. Laura and Sandy were reading *Tom Sawyer*. Laura explained that she usually read one paragraph and Sandy would read the next paragraph.

Although the family has not questioned her ability, it once was questioned by the school. In one of Laura's letters to me, there was a brief paragraph that focused on the results of some reading tests that Sarah, Beth, and Sandy had taken in school. Laura wrote,

> My children just brought home their comprehensive tests of basic skills results from school. Sandy got such a low score in one phase of reading, I think there was a mistake. In sentence comprehension she got 35% while vocabulary was 95% and reading passage comprehension was 88%. I'll have to go ask what that means. Is my kid a freak? The percents mean National Percentile Rank. Of course, I say the test is freaked out, not my kid.

I asked Laura what she meant by "Is my kid a freak?" Did she wonder if Sandy had some problem with sentence comprehension? She replied immediately,

> No, of course not. I said it tongue in cheek. I was questioning the school. There's no doubt in my mind. It's just one more indication to me that what they are doing is mechanistic and has nothing to do with the real world.

Upon entering fourth grade Sandy was accepted into a program for the academically talented.

For some children, however, failure is more than merely an option; it is the only alternative. While teaching in a clinical situation, I worked with a white, eleven-year-old boy who was unable to read. Jack had been retained in the third grade of a parochial school and was likely to be retained for another year. When I spoke with the teacher, she said he could not keep up with his third-grade assignments, and then added that he would be better with second-grade texts, but unfortunately that would mean joining a second-grade class. Jack came to the reading lessons with his mother. He was eager to learn and made surprising progress during the first four weeks of lessons— and then he quit. He came each week, but showed no interest in the activities, and while the others in his group made steady progress, Jack regressed to his previous level. Nothing motivated him. At the final meeting, Jack's father came with him and we talked. Not knowing the circumstances, I spoke of Jack's sudden change of heart. His father leaned forward and said he had told Jack not to get so excited if he could not read, and then he added that Jack was like him, and that he could not read either. Although it is possible that Jack had some primary reading problem inherited from his father, his progress and his father's subsequent comments would seem to indicate that his change of heart was exactly that. His father told him that he could not learn to read and so he gave up.

BUILDING RELATIONAL CONTEXTS

If Sandy Lindell did not want to read, then her parents read to her. She listened to stories. She wrote notes and letters and drew pictures. She received notes from her family and did her chores according to the list taped to the refrigerator door. For Sandy, as with the other children, reading and writing were activities to be shared. They were meaningful, concrete tasks dictated in many ways by the social setting, literate events that occurred as a part of family life, a way of building and maintaining the relational contexts of everyday life.

The degree to which literacy is embedded in the social processes of family life is well illustrated by the comments of Jessie Dawson, who offered the following description of an evening she had shared with Hannah and Ellie.

> The other night Ellie and I bought a copy of *Peter Rabbit* in French for Hannah, to put in her stocking (for Christmas) because we wanted to have a toy or something. And Hannah has always loved *Peter Rabbit*, so we had it out here and we were looking at it trying to decide whether Ellie should have it because she just started taking French or whether we should really give it to Hannah. Hannah came in from dancing class and said, "Oh my goodness, French *Peter Rabbit*" and picked it up and we both said to her, "Well, Merry Christmas to you." Everyone was tired. Hannah has decided she's old enough to date; we've decided she isn't. Great constant conflict and very few close moments; it's a real pulling away. And she sat down with it and she

opened it up and began looking through it and she said, "Look, the pictures are exactly the same." We always keep *Peter Rabbit* right here, so we got the English and we read a page and then she read a page and the next thing we knew we were going through all the *Peter Rabbit* books, and when we looked up Dan had gone to bed hours ago. It was twenty minutes to eleven and we were reading *Peter Rabbit*, curled up on the couch, the three of us. What a marvelous evening that was, to go back all the way back to the age of three or four, and it was just a wonderful time.

Jessie grinned and said, "I don't know what in the world you can do with information like that but it's a memory that I shall carry for a long time." We talked for a while of fifteen year olds and Jessie explained:

> You'd want to sit next to her and have a cup of tea and you'd have to have this conversation, "Why can't I wear blue eye shadow?" That's more important than anything else, and this erased everything and we went all the way back. It was a marvelous evening. Also at this age they shun physical affection although they still need some, and you have to tease them into it a bit. Just to be able to give them a kiss now and then. That night I tucked her into bed and she said, "Goodnight." She didn't say, "Oh, mother!" It was gone just for that night. To be able to go back.

The rarified atmosphere of the evening that Jessie shared with Hannah and Ellie may never be repeated, but in telling the tale, Jessie vividly illustrates the extent to which the seemingly benign literate activity of reading bedtime stories to the preschool child can permeate years of family life. Steeped in memories of the past, they found understanding in the present through the temporal integration of their experience.

For Jessie, literacy was the medium for sharing something special with her daughter, but literacy can also be the contrivance of the dissent that sometimes separates mother and child. During a study (Taylor, 1978b) that examined the coping strategies and social support systems of nonliterate adults, Myra, a black senior citizen, spoke of her family experience of growing up unable to read and write, and the determination with which she pursued the education of her five children. Her account is presented in full since it is a very powerful description of the discontinuities that the pursuit of literacy can create.

> I grew up and found that education was needed. Two things—God and education. I put my back against the wall. I said I would never have kids and not try to let them read. And I try and

I come up and I have five kids and I sent them to school and gave them a good education. But after the kids then come up and find then that I couldn't read they didn't care for me. But my oldest daughter came to this country and she sent for me and she bring me and when I came she said that, "I'll take you from your country to live, to let you leave those kids because I see they don't care for you." Two was from the first husband and three was from the second husband. But the second children didn't care. The first care. When my eldest daughter came here she keep writing and then she says, "I'm going to take you, I'm going to take you because I want you to put a pencil on a piece of paper." And then I come here in '69 she brings me to this school here. The teacher was Mrs. Oh I forget her name right now, but I think she was the teacher Mrs.—I forgot the teacher's name. And she said, "This is my mother" that is she is the only one that would say that is she, that I'm the mother. And I bring all these children here. After she brought me I work and she keep on telling me, "I want you to read, I want you to put a pencil on paper and read because you learned us to read you know," she said "get started."

There was a high school in my country. And in my country, you know, you have to pay for everything there. You get nothing free. I work and send them through high school. And in my country when you go through high school you can get any job there. So after my eldest daughter brought me she take me to, I can't remember the teacher's name, she's in California now, and she tell her, she said, "This is my mother." She tell her everything what I told you. She said, "I want her to read." But after having all those kids in my country that were in high school, and the boy was going to college, I couldn't give them up. She wanted me to give them up but I couldn't. Because they were my children. She said I don't want you to work. I want you to go to school, to learn to read and write because you know it is important. So she brought me here, you know and I come now and then. When I can. Until I got those children where they was. But after I brought them here they didn't count me no more because I couldn't read or write. They go their way.

I forgive them you know. But I don't forget them. What they do. Because even my son when he was living here, if I ask him a word, he said, "don't have any time." And if I asked my daughter, "What is this word?" she hardly tell me. She said, "I don't have the time." It hurts. When you try and give up half your life for the kids. I could do bad by them. I could give them away—just toss them away. But I didn't.

And my daughter said the same thing, "If you go when I take you in '69 you would be a good reader and writer now. But you help all those kids and you see they didn't pay you now." But now, you know, they pay me a little mind because they know I'm going to school. But I guess I won't bother with them. Every time they call me I answer them nice and good and when they come I appreciate them, but, you know, I don't have too much to do with them. Understand. (Taylor, 1978b, pp 7–8)

Whatever other factors were involved in her family problems, Myra perceived the fact that she could not read and write as the major reason why she was not accepted by her children. She was a victim of literacy. While Jessie spoke of literacy as enhancing her relationship with her children, Myra identified literacy as the stumbling block that separated her from her children. Literacy can, it seems, make or break the relational contexts of family life.

LITERACY, SOCIAL STATUS, AND IDENTITY

If "both status and identity are developed in daily interactions" (McDermott, 1976, p. 399), then literacy, as the integration of talking and listening and reading and writing, could be viewed as setting the conditions for a variety of social practices. Here the experiences of the families are filtered through the comments of several of the nonliterate adults who participated in Taylor's illiteracy study to emphasize the degree to which literate social practices shape both status and identity.

Discussing the difficulties she faced, Myra spoke of her distress when her only means of communicating with her family had been through letters written for her by nonfamily members. At the time of the conversation, Myra was beginning to write her own letters, and she commented on this new development:

> When I want to write to my family. My sisters. I have two sisters there. When I want to write them. This is very difficult. But now I can write them. You know, I don't write them a long letter. I write them a couple of lines. And they understand it—a little. (Taylor, 1978b, p. 8)

In the same study, other areas of difficulty were noted by Ernie, who was in his mid-forties. Ernie had grown up in the South. His mother died when he was five, leaving his father with six children. Ernie's nine-year-old sister assumed the maternal role of caring for the children; she was also responsible for the cooking and cleaning. When Ernie was fourteen his father died and the children were left to cope as best they could. Ernie talked of attending school until he was in the fifth grade, but he explained that he was never there long enough to understand what was going on. Similarly, Ernie's wife had never learned to read. He described how the school had been twelve miles from her home and therefore she had never managed to attend on a regular basis.

Among the difficulties Ernie spoke of were the problems he experienced when traveling. He spoke of coping with street names. He would have the word written on a piece of paper, and he would try to match it with the street name. With unmistakable sincerity, he added that it was no good if the first letter matched, that did not mean it was the right word. The whole word had to match. Another difficulty was being able to prove that the items he owned really belonged to him. He pointed to the ring I was wearing, and he repeated several times how important it was for me to be able to prove the ring was mine. Ernie went on to talk of the house he was buying; he had to rely on friends to tell him that the house was legally his.

Although Ernie faced these immense problems on a daily basis, they did not compare with the formidable task of finding employment. Ernie spoke of the application forms for his present job. He explained:

> I sat in school and the teacher helped me fill in the application. Well, it wasn't bad. Getting it was bad. But she showed me and it wasn't too bad. I filled it out at school and she showed me. So when I went to the job I filled it out again on my own and so I passed and so I got the job.

Writing letters to family and friends, reading signs, demonstrating ownership, and filling out forms were all functional literate activities for the children participating in the study. From a very young age, print formed one medium for mediating experience. Before the children could read and write in the traditional sense, they were writing letters. Debbie Farley's birthday "Hello" and Steven Langdon's letter of circles and lines are both relevant examples of such letters. Navigating by reading signs began in the backpack: "Pizza," "Exit," and "Two Guys" were quickly learned as visual symbols of purposeful activities. Designating ownership began with the children's names, often written on the pictures they drew, and filling in forms became a more noticeable activity as print became a more prominent aspect of their increasingly sophisticated play.

Thus the children are growing in familial contexts; the parents' literate habits infuse their children's lives with literate activities. Although the passage from home to school marked a shift in emphasis from function to form, literacy remained a highly valued prize. The children moved from one literate environment to another with the minimum of difficulty. Ernie's four children were not so fortunate. He spoke briefly of how bright and eager his children had seemed when they were little, but that as they had grown, they had "lost it." Ernie described the conversations he had with his children when they were little. Speaking with affection and a certain disappointment, he explained:

> I told them when I was coming up there wasn't no opportunity. Today opportunity is knocking on people's doors—and so take advantage of it. I told them I would try college, 'cause you get one year and the door get a little open. And you get two years and the door open a little wider, three years, well you go four and the door is going to open for you. I want to send my boy to college, he don't want to go. I want to send my daughter to college but she don't want to go. So what they did. Them got jobs. Two of them are working. My son is making windows in schools. That's something he likes to do. He's doing that. My daughter she's working on a newspaper. Kind of newspaper she's working on in a factory. So she likes that.

CONCLUSIONS

For the families participating in the field research, literacy is a part of the very fabric of family life. Southgate (1972) defines literacy as "the mastery of our native language in all its aspects, as a means of communication" (p. 9). This is an apt way of describing the anticipated consequences of the early literate experiences of the children participating in the study. Growing in an environment where literacy is the only option, they learned of reading as one way of listening, and of writing as one way of talking. Literacy gave the children both status and identity as it became the medium of shared experience; it facilitated the temporal integration of their social histories as the highly valued artifact of family life became the prized commodity of the schools. Clearly, children from such literate environments have an enormous advantage in learning to read and write, for as Vygotsky (1978) states, the mastery of print does indeed herald a critical turning point in their cultural lives.

Such experiences are beyond the reach of many children, and the possibility exists that literacy will emerge in their lives not only as a barrier between home and school but also as a contrivance of familial dissent. The comments of several nonliterate adults illustrate Mead's comments on the discontinuities which are created for so many people by our modern education system. These are examples of some of the difficulties faced by adults and children with minimal literacy skills.

Considering literacy in this cultural context emphasizes the need for educators to question seriously whether the present adult literacy programs and parent educational programs tend to be too literally literate. It is entirely possible that the undue emphasis on specific didactic encounters might unwittingly undermine the opportunity for reading and writing to become socially significant in the lives of both adults and children, and therefore an integral facet of family life. In this context the recommendations of Hunter and Harman (1979) should be given serious consideration. In their report on adult illiteracy in the United States, these authors contend that only 2 to 4 percent of nonliterate adults participate in existing programs because the programs are not immediately relevant to their everyday lives. Hunter and Harman stress the need for a network of community-based literacy programs designed in part by the participants. If such a plan was operationalized, the spillover to the children of parents with minimal literacy skills could be substantial; it seems reasonable to assume that if literacy becomes socially significant in the lives of the parents, it is likely to become socially significant in the lives of the children.

6

Family Literacy
and Learning in School

Unlike the teaching of spoken language, into which children grow up on their own accord, teaching of written language is based on artificial training. Such training requires an enormous amount of attention and effort on the part of teacher and pupil and thus becomes something self-contained, relegating living written language to the background. Instead of being founded on the needs of children as they naturally develop and on their own activity, writing is given to them from without, from the teacher's hand. (Vygotsky, 1978, p. 105)

At a recent ethnograpic research forum, Scribner (1980) made the sobering comment that not every study leads to implications for practice. In addition, we are often guilty of stretching the implications of our findings when, as Leichter and Mitchell state, "The scope of any single investigation is necessarily limited (when) compared with the knowledge needs of the practitioner" (1978, p. 301). The importance of qualitative research is not the discovery of some particular practical manipulation, but the questions it raises; in developing new understandings of the local and distinctive meanings and uses of literacy in the lives of people, we may come a little closer to appreciating some of the assumptions (both good and bad) that form the basis of our present pedagogies of reading and writing. However, in this study I have also tried to view the researcher's questions from the perspective of the practitioner. In this chapter I present my findings together with other views of family literacy in exploring possible ways of introducing reading and writing to children, so these activities will have some social significance in their everyday lives.

One might say that the children in this study learned and are learning to read and write in liberating ways; literacy enables them to participate fully in the social system of which they are a part. There are, however, many ways children can learn of print. Writing of liberating literacy, Cremin states, "But whether one is encouraged to become literate in the liberating sense can depend in large measure on the context in which one is educated" (1970, p. 549). Riesman is more explicit. He speaks of children being "forced into slavery to print through parental fanaticism or pedagogues' pressures" (1955, p. 16).

Some children must indeed be enslaved, but others, by "failing" to learn to read and write, have resisted capture. These children are the true victims of literacy.

We cannot assume that children growing up in any specific setting learn or do not learn of the uses of print in their preschool years. Most of us know of middle-class homes where print is noticeably absent and of working class homes littered with papers and books. Many children in our society begin their elementary school education with no appreciation of the functional utility of the print in their environment. Many children have had little opportunity to develop reading and writing as interpersonal language skills which complement and reinforce speaking and listening as interrelated forms of a communicative system. Nevertheless, reading and writing are lifted out of context in schools and become the focus of specific, culturally remote pedagogical attention. Literacy becomes an end in itself, reduced to a hierarchy of interrelated skills, when, as Ferreiro so cogently states, "The process by which a child arrives at an understanding of a particular type of representation of spoken language, e.g., alphabetical writing, cannot be reduced to the establishment of a series of habits and skills however complex" (1978, p. 26). My findings support Ferreiro's position and emphasize that a skills approach to literacy runs counter to the natural development of reading and writing as complex cultural activities.

This circumstance can be most easily appreciated by considering the alphabetic paradox referred to by Gough (1972) as an "infamous fact." In "The Cooperative Research Program in FirstGrade Reading Instruction," Bond and Dykstra (1967) report that knowledge of the alphabet is the single best predictor of reading achievement. Samuels (1971) points out that no studies have found evidence that specifically teaching the alphabet facilitates learning to read. Gough's "infamous fact" has a hint of logicality about it, for it raises the question of whether the children who knew the alphabet were ever taught in the traditional sense of the word, and if they were never taught, then why should other children profit by such instruction? The children participating in the present research resisted any such instruction, and yet they all learned the alphabet as they came to use print in the mediation of their experiences of one another.

Within this context the writings of Vygotsky (1978) become important, and the question emerges of whether we can seriously expect children who have never experienced or have limited experience of reading and writing as complex cultural activities to successfully learn to read and write from the narrowly defined pedagogical practices of our schools. Can we teach children on an individual level of intrapersonal processes what they have never experienced on a social level as interpersonal processes of functional utility in their everyday lives? I would submit that we cannot.

The research of Istomina, which supports the position of Vygotsky on the internalization of higher psychological functions, further supports this viewpoint. Istomina was concerned with the questions of when and under what conditions voluntary recall and voluntary attention first emerge in young children. In a series of experiments and observations of children in play situations, Istomina found support for the working hypothesis that during the preschoolage period, memory processes (recall, retention) are integrated into some other activity and are not voluntary. Istomina contends that it is only later that these processes are transformed into "specific, integral acts." Speaking of the preschool children participating in the research, he states, "When a child was given the task of memorizing or recalling something that had no intrinsic relation to what he was doing, to his immediate situation, and to his active desires, he was unable to cope with the task" (1948, p. 15).

If one subscribes to the position that the activities of young children must have some intrinsic relationship to their immediate situation, then the idea that reading and writing should be taught as a series of skills (the traditional approach) becomes less palatable. Children in the present study learned of print through a whole language process; while learning to talk, they learned of the social significance of such signs as "Two Guys" and "Exit," played with the reinvention of letters and words, and experimented with "reading" stories. Such a miscellany perhaps led Vygotsky to speak of development as "a complex dialectical process characterized by periodicity, unevenness in development of different functions, metamorphosis or qualitative transformation of one form into another intertwining of external factors, and adaptive processes" (1978, p. 73).

If such a view of literate language learning is accepted, then how should young children be taught to read? When I asked the parents participating in the study how their children learned, they were unable to answer. They emphasized the importance of the activities in the home and particularly noted the reading of bedtime stories, but they were unable to say exactly how it had happened. When I asked Joe King how Bonnie had learned, he replied, "She just put it all together." When I asked Nina Simms how Carol had learned, she said, "She just did it," and then added, "There were things in the house and she just learned." I then asked the parents "who fails?" Their overwhelming response was children who are not interested in learning to read and write. Lee Farley said that children fail because "no one ever considered it important." Leo Langdon talked of children failing "who are not motivated to read," and Nina Simms spoke of children who are not interested "because nobody is interested." The parents' emphasis on motivation is echoed in the literature (Bar-Tal, 1978), and it is, of course, one answer to the question of "who fails?" However, it is entirely possible that many children "fail" because they never have the opportunity to experience the diffuse, moment-to-moment uses of print—the learning experiences of which the parents found it so difficult to speak. Print is presented to them as some abstract decontextualized phenomenon unrelated to their everyday lives. They learn of reading as a private affair, something that happens in the workbook pages of impractical notions where teachers and children meet.

In the literature, this perspective is supported by Hale who writes of a two-year study of teachers listening to children read. Hale found that in this situation, reading was equated with producing acceptable verbalizations through decoding a given text. She states, "It was the connection between visual symbols and sound which was regarded as problematic, and correct verbalization was normally taken to be a measure of comprehension" (1980, p. 26). Hale goes on to stress that the children learned in a social situation where reading development was defined as "beyond the control of the child." It was implicit to the occasion that progress depended upon "the adoption of particular rules of procedure with teacher direction and reinforcement" (p. 27). The point is that all children begin school endowed with highly complex communicative systems (McDermott, 1976, 1978; Anderson, 1977; Labov, 1979). However, some children's communication systems do not prepare them for learning to read and write in the traditional sense. The difficulties go much deeper. Many of the programs designed to sensitize parents to their role as teachers of reading and writing provide them with specific suggestions on the "how to" of reading instruction, yet there is nothing in the literature to suggest that children who successfully learn to read and write are specifically taught by their parents. The present research seriously questions the degree to which such tutelage takes place. In the families participating in this study, literacy is deeply embedded in the social processes of family life and is not some specific list of activities added to the family agenda to explicitly teach reading. The thin literate veneer of present programming cannot substitute for such learning opportunities and may not necessarily be desirable (Szwed, 1977), for it may "unwittingly undermine the 'natural' and 'exploratory' educational initiatives of the child" (Leichter, 1978, p. 621) as well as the initiatives that the parents and children have evolved together.

The present research emphasizes the naiveté of attempts to simulate literate learning, while at the same time stressing the urgent need of building relational contexts which will enable all children to use print in the mediation of their relationships. McDermott states, "The important question to be asked is whether the subject matter is introduced in the proper relational contexts" (1977, p. 176). The implicit question is whether relational contexts can be built within the classroom so that reading instruction, as it is presently thought of, can become a meaningful enterprise. (See also McDermott, 1978.) Only when children have had the opportunity to inventively construct literate language uses which make sense to them will they be able to participate fully in literate society.

The research imperative is unquestionable. To facilitate literate learning, we need to know more of the ways that children from a variety of social settings initiate, absorb, and synthesize the educational influences in their environment (Leichter, 1978, p. 240). The search is not for negative habits but for positive actions. Kavale states, "Illiterate adults have avoided situations where reading or writing is required. These negative habits must be extinguished and replaced by positive attitudes and behaviors" (1977, p. 371). Kavale's avoidance strategies and negative habits might be viewed as positive actions, as ways of overcoming the lack of literacy skills through the development of coping strategies and social support systems which enable the nonliterate person to function in society (Taylor, 1978b).

We need to know more of the learning styles, coping strategies, and social support systems of the children we teach if instruction in reading and writing is to be a meaningful complement to their lives. Fortunately, there are researchers, working in a variety of disciplines and using many different research techniques, engaged in research which may eventually provide this information. Excellent examples of such research are the studies of Anderson, Teale, and Estrada (1980); Au (1980); Bissex (1980); Harste, Burke, and Woodward (1981); Scribner and Cole (1981); Sulzby (1981); and especially Paley (1981). Paley has recorded conversations, stories, and play acting of her kindergarten class, and she has used the magic of their thinking to present a remarkable perspective of the language and thought of five-year-old children. From tooth fairies and bad witches to lions that roar, Paley shares her children's world, growing with them as they explore ideas and develop new understandings of themselves and their world. Paley's is a straightforward text. She has no sophisticated research design to complicate her task, just the power of naturalistic observations. Her approach has much to offer to researchers and teachers who are interested in creating comfortable academic settings for children.

TEACHING CHILDREN
FROM DIVERSE SOCIAL SITUATIONS TO READ AND WRITE

Children need to explore the uses of print before they are specifically taught to read and write, and many children are unprepared for the present pedagogical practices of our schools. In addition, there is an urgent need to establish relational contexts so children from diverse social situations can learn reading and writing as meaningful complements to their cultural heritage.

The emphasis on specific didactic approaches to teaching reading and writing may unwittingly undermine any opportunity for reading and writing to become socially significant in the lives of those we teach. There are indirect benefits to the children of families participating in neighborhood literacy programs such as those advocated by Hunter and Harman (1979). But how can we help the children more directly? Swzed emphasizes that attempts to change home practices, "even with the best intentions, are not easily accomplished and not necessarily desirable" (1977, p. 11). The serious ethical difficulties of family intervention programs, together with the sociological and political impracticality (Hale, 1980) of any attempts to change reading instructions in school, leaves few alternatives. One approach which deserves serious consideration is the development of carefully planned, public and cooperative literate learning environments for prekindergarten and kindergarten children; in these environments children can learn the functions of print before they are introduced to the abstract literate activities of first-grade classrooms. This does not imply a return to the progressive movement of the 1960s, but as the British Committee of Inquiry states in the Bullock Report, *A Language for Life*, "There is no question of waiting for readiness to occur; for with many children it does not come 'naturally' and must be brought about by the teacher's positive measures to induce it" (1975, p. 102). The emphasis is on "induction not instruction" (HunterGrundin, 1979), with "natural" methods of teaching reading and writing involving "appropriate operations on the child's environment" (Vygotsky, 1978, p. 118). Thus, the prekindergarten and kindergarten years would become a complex phase of transition designed to lead the children from their homes and into first-grade classrooms as they learn of print in social situations which have immediate relevance to their lives.

Many useful suggestions for helping children to appreciate the social significance of written language are contained in the writings of Clay (1972), Forester (1975), Forester and Mickelson (1979), and Hunter-Grundin (1979). However, these ideas are still based on school models of learning. Somehow we need to bridge the gap between home and school so that reading in the one is reading in the other (Taylor, 1982). One opportunity to make the quantum leap is suggested by Holdaway (1979, p. 148). He uses the sociolinguistic research of Halliday (1973) to bring the functions and uses of print into the classroom. Holdaway summarizes Halliday's categories as follows:

Instrumental	The "I want" function	Fulfilling needs
Regulatory	The "Don't do that" function	Controlling
Interactional	The "I love you" function	Relating to others
Personal	The "This is me" function	Defining self
Heuristic	The "What's that?" function	Finding out
Imaginative	The "Let's pretend" function	Making believe
Representational	The "This is how it is" function	Communicating about content

Holdaway builds a multifunctional literacy program that translates everyday uses of print into workable classroom practices. Although he is critical of present practices, he does not disregard the extraordinary advances that were made during the 1970s. His book is, in many ways, an interpretation of the decade by a creative and imaginative teacher who is sensitive to the need for researchers to examine "the meaning of meaning" in the popular definition of reading as the meaningful interpretation of written or printed symbols. Within this context Holdaway brings Halliday's multifunctional view of meaning to the development of literacy skills and values. Halliday writes:

> For the child, all language is doing something; in other words it is meaning. It has meaning in a very broad sense, including here a range of functions which the adult does not normally think of as meaningful, such as the personal and the interactional. . . But it is precisely in relation to the child's conception of language that it is most vital for us to redefine our notion of meaning; not restricting it to the narrow limits of representational meaning (that is, "content") *but including within it all the functions that language has as a purposive, non-random, contextualized activity* (1973, pp. 17–18).

We need to redefine our notion of meaning to include all the functions that literacy has "as a purposive, non-random, contextualized activity." To do so, we must reach out into the communities where we teach and bring the functions and uses of print into our classrooms. Billboards and flyers, letters and newspapers, price tags and street signs all have a place in classrooms.

Holdaway takes the sharing of stories as the cornerstone of his multifunctional literacy program. The universal appeal of sharing stories makes it the most important component of any functional literacy program. In each of the families participating in the field research, reading stories was an integral part of their lives; both parents and children spoke of the stories they shared as important precursors of literacy (Taylor, 1980). Sandy Lindell said:

> When I wanted to read I said to my mother "Why can't I read?" And she said, "I don't know why." So she just read me books and got interested and so my father kept reading me books. That's how it happened.

In the literature, the importance of reading stories has been emphasized by Bamberger (1974) and Britton (1970); in the Bullock Report, the British Committee of Inquiry (1975) concludes that there is a priority need to introduce children to books in their preschool years. In addition, researchers have studied the positive effect of reading stories on reading achievement (Cohen, 1968) and on linguistic development (Chomsky, 1969; Strickland, 1971). The advocacy of reading to children, however, has a much longer history. Aries writes of seventeenth and eighteenth century paintings and engravings depicting the storyteller or charlatan perched on a platform "telling his story and pointing with a stick to the text written on a big board" (1962, p. 97). In 1862, while teaching at Yasnaya Polyana, Tolstoy wrote of the first "rational and immutable" method of teaching reading. It consisted of the teacher reading as a mother would read with her child, and thus Tolstoy called it the "domestic method." He states:

> In spite of all means which are supposed to mechanize instruction and presumably facilitate the work of the teacher with a large number of pupils, this method will always remain the best and only one for teaching people to read and read fluently. (1967, p. 264)

Some forty-six years later, Huey expressed the opinion that "the secret of it all lies in parents' reading aloud to and with the children" (1908, p. 332).

There is currently a revival in story reading in schools, and storytellers are once again receiving recognition. The fact that many children are listening to stories for the first time is emphasized by Hill who speaks of children "starved of stories" in the workingclass communities of London, and of their craving for stories which one would have thought they had outgrown. Hill writes:

> Many of the children we meet are obviously starved of stories. There is something sad about this. I remember the first year we began storytelling. I had consciously chosen unfamiliar rather tough stories after looking round the parks at our potential audience. Walking through Brixton one day I was stopped by a waiflike girl of about ten. "Will you tell us Cinderella in the Brockwell Park next week?" she said. It might be reasonable to suppose that a ten year old would have had a surfeit of the most familiar stories like Cinderella, and would have reached the stage of needing something more sophisticated. But so many of the children we meet in Lambeth have missed out on an essential stage of childhood. No one at home has ever told them stories, hence the fact that they still long to hear Cinderella at the age of ten. (1974, pp. 99–100)

Watching the storytellers in Central Park, New York, one can see the enormous impact their stories have on their audience. Shopping-bag ladies, little children, and roller skaters listen with bated breath as the storyteller "paints pictures with the sound of words" (Farnsworth, 1978).

There are many ways the sharing of stories could be incorporated into functional literacy programs for prekindergarten and kindergarten children, making books a meaningful complement to their social heritage. As Holdaway so cogently states, "if the human richness and joy of a fine literature could be moved across into the center of literacy teaching, many of the problems of cultural dissonance might be minimized" (1979, p. 17). If provisions were made for children to share stories with significant members of their own communities, they would have the opportunity to "read" along, possibly reaching a stage when they would be free to experiment with the words of the text in telling the tale. These are ways of providing children with socially significant experiences of print. Perhaps, it is only after children have shared stories and experienced reading and writing as complex cultural activities that they will be able to learn on an individual level through the traditional pedagogical practices of the first-grade classroom.

7

Fieldwork Approaches to the Study of Literacy and the Family

Neither means nor ends are absolute: the end sought is not an ultimate destination but a temporary resting place: the means to it is not something merely to be traversed but itself partakes of the value in the journey. (Kaplan, 1964, p. 116)

In their study of culture at a distance, Mead and Metraux write of the relationship between "the idiosyncratic style of the research worker, the record of the work in progress, and the types of results that emerge" (1953, p. 7). This chapter explores that relationship.

THE SPIRIT OF ETHNOGRAPHY

In recent years, many researchers in the field of education have come to question traditional research paradigms, there is an increasing insistence on adopting alternative approaches to the study of education. In a paper that focuses on meaning in context, Mishler writes:

> Questions that had been settled once and for all by scientific revolution reappear to haunt and bedevil us. The scientific method was to be our guarantor of objectivity and neutrality; diligent application of its rigorous procedures was, in turn, to produce a body of cumulative knowledge that was systematic and general. (1979, p. 17)

Mishler concludes that it has not worked out that way. Magoon's paper on constructivism carries a similar message, but the language is more explicit. He states, "Schooling, teaching and learning go on without being extricable via traditional approaches, and serious doubts about methodology have been raised publicly within the research community" (1977, p. 653).

Similar discontent has been voiced in the reading field. In 1974, the editors of the *Reading Research Quarterly*, Farr and Weintraub, spoke of the many "well-designed, carefully implemented, and precisely documented studies related to reading," which they contend are "narrow in scope and fail to address themselves to the most important issues and concerns related to understanding the reading process." Wolf and Tymitz (1976) have since added to the debate by contending that traditional research paradigms are "restrictive" and "esoteric." These are strong sentiments, but they are used effectively by these authors to emphasize the need for alternative approaches to reading research. Farr and Weintraub state:

> We are sorely in need of research designs and new approaches that allow variables to emerge from the situation being studied, that admit to a lack of answers and even to a lack of questions, that allow for study in a natural setting, and that provide for the researcher's biases as well as alternative interpretations. (n.p.)

Wolf and Tymitz extend this argument by specifically advocating ethnographic research. They write, "Because it is essentially an issue generative approach, the potential exists for new insights and questions to emerge which have been beyond the scope of our current methodology" (n.p.).

Ethnography, the foundation of anthropological research since Boaz in the United States and Malinowsky in England, has become the "grand idée" (Langer, 1960) of educational (and reading) researchers. It is an idea of recent fame, and like all new ideas, it has burst forth as a cure-all for the maladies afflicting the body politic of educational research. However, the increasing popularity of ethnographic research is viewed with alarm by many anthropologists. Birdwhistell says that the words "that have been useful tools for one generation can, and often do, become icons or cliché forms in the hands of another" (1977, p.103), and he goes on to note that many students use the word ethnography in a very different way than his contemporaries. Rist (1980), in a paper with the canny title "Blitzkrieg Ethnography: On the Transformation of a Method into a Movement," writes of the mutation of the epistemological underpinnings of ethnographic research and of its methodological applications. He, unlike Birdwhistell, ends on a positive note by concluding that, although there have been costs, the increased popularity of ethnography has led to the expansion of methods with new techniques and new audiences. He states, "The use of ethnography is now, more than ever, institutionalized as a viable tool for the research community." (p. 10)

Talking about the "openness of meanings," Kaplan writes of "terms which require for a specification of their meaning not one sentential context but the context of the whole set of sentences in which they occur" (1964, p. 64). Kaplan speaks of "systemic meaning" stating, "Each sentential occurrence is a partial determination of the meaning, but only as we encounter the terms in more and more

contexts of varying sorts do we come to understand it more fully"
(p. 64). Literacy is such a term, and ethnography is another. Both
defy simple definition. Signification evolves as the research proceeds,
and the evolution of these terms marks the passage of science.

In 1928, Maragaret Mead published *Coming of Age in Samoa*, a
study of Samoan adolescence. This was soon followed by *Growing up
in New Guinea*, in which Mead wrote of the Manus tribe of the
Admiralty Islands. Both texts, classics in the field of anthropology,
are ethnographic accounts of primitive peoples. A quarter of a century later, Mead writes of these works:

> We had learned, just learned, that we could gain much from the
> disciplined study of primitive people, that there was a priceless
> laboratory in which we could investigate the possibilities inher-
> ent in human nature. Exploration of the ways of life of savages,
> as materials for art, for philosophy, for history, was not new. *But
> the calculated use of a primitive culture to throw light on contemporary
> problems was new.* (1956, p.9; emphasis added)

Ethnography brought primitive culture to the civilized world. In
these early descriptions, we learned of the rites of passage, rituals,
and routines of far-off people, and by exploring their living, lov-
ing, fighting, eating, sleeping, and dying, we were able to pierce the
hide of our own culture and look more closely at ourselves. As the
years passed, there was an increasing recognition that a new and
equally priceless laboratory existed in our own backyards. Ethnography enables us to study contemporary culture. Exemplary of such endeavors are Gans's (1962) study of class, culture, and social structure
of Italian-Americans (*Urban Villagers*), Goffman's (1971) research of
face-to-face interactions in public places (*Relations in Public*), Shuttles's
(1968) investigation of ethnicity and territory in the inner city (*The
Social Order of the Slum*), and Varenne's (1977) delineation of the roles
of individualism, community, and love in a small midwestern town
(*Americans Together*).

In recent years, as ethnography has developed as a science, many
divergent and disputed paths have been taken (Berreman, 1972).
Central to the ethnographic endeavor, however, is the search for
structures of signification in the behavior of others. The essential
components are the constructions of the informants reconstructed
with the researcher into representations in their own right. Geertz
(1973) refers to these metaphorical manipulations when, using the
original meaning of fiction, he speaks of anthropological writings as
"fictions." It is not that they are false or unfactual, but that they are

"something made" or "something fashioned." From this perspective, ethnography is neither theory nor method, nor is it boundary specific. Geertz defines it as a certain kind of intellectual effort which he describes as an elaborate venture in "thick description." It seems that ethnography is simply a well-formed language providing insights into the lives of others. My research aspires to such a language in its attempt to capture on paper a fleeting reflection of one aspect of the informants' lives; as such it might kindly be referred to as field research undertaken in the spirit of ethnography.

Images of the Researcher

Traditionally, the researcher working with informants begins in ignorance. She brings with her a personal philosophy of science, a theoretical perspective, and methods of obtaining data, but she does not know how the informants construct their world. The informants hold all the cards. The researcher is the neophyte, seeking knowledge and information (Spradley, 1979). In matters of the family and literacy, however, the researcher is no neophyte. In fact, this area might well be considered familiar, for she belongs to a family and has achieved some degree of literacy. Woven into the fabric of her existence, familiarity becomes the major difficulty of the research endeavor. Herein lies the paradox, for as a member of the social system, the researcher knows a lot about the family and literacy, and yet, as a member of a scientific community, she knows very little about the familial contexts in which young children learn to read and write. And so, she watches, listens, and asks questions as interviews fade into conversations of shared experiences in which impulses, instincts, feelings, and hunches help construct schemes of analysis which must be reorganized as new data are obtained. As Varenne so aptly states, "In the relationship observer-observed there is no fixed point, everything is in continuous motion" (1977, p. 224).

Bateson emphasizes that "just as the objective record of fieldwork must be examined in detail, so also the personal aspects should be understood" (1980, p.273). Clearly, in research studies that rely so heavily on the researcher's presentation of self in the field, some examination of the significant personal experiences which shaped her perceptions must be included in the research report. Such conscious awareness of one's self is difficult (if not impossible) to achieve, and, at best, all I can offer is an account of some of the thoughts that passed through my mind as I addressed the issue of my personal contribution to the research project.

Much of who I am is tied up with the fact that I am English and, until recently, a visitor to the United States. The families participating in the study were aware of my Englishness, but they showed it in different ways. Donna King identified with my transitory state, for she considered herself a Californian. Donna sometimes talked about the differences between West Coast and East Coast living, and once she commented that life in the Northeast was probably as foreign to her as it was to me. One day when I invited Nina Simms and her family to my home, she told me of an English friend who used to invite them to her house where she would serve them afternoon tea in beautiful bone china. Nina, Azar, Carol, and Andrew came to "Sunday tea," a ritual we had left behind in England but gladly reinstated for the occasion. We ate tiny sandwiches and cream cakes, experimented with pots of various teas, and talked of forgotten customs as we watched the children (including my own) who were much impressed by the ceremonious event.

One of the ways that being English played a part in my relationship with the families was the momentary interruptions in conversations when I used words or phrases which marked my foreignness. Once Nina Simms and I talked about the finicky eating habits of our children, and I commented that my children preferred "shop cake." The conversation stopped abruptly as Nina frowned at me and said, "What kind?" and then added, "Store bought, right?" I replied, "From the store," and the conversation continued as Nina laughingly bemoaned her children's preference for Burger King fast food. Other ways that my Englishness was acknowledged by the families and by myself passed unnoticed but are recognizable in the transcripts of the conversations. Being English and American comes through in the stories we told each other, for the parents, in telling me of their childhood memories, recounted not only events from their past but also what it was like to grow up in the United States in an age that is beyond my experience of American life. The tales I told of my early years held more than a fleeting glimpse of a post-war England that has vanished forever.

In retrospect, the fact that I am English not only greatly affected the kinds of information I obtained but also facilitated the special role I tried to maintain. In conceptualizing the role of the researcher, Pelto and Pelto state:

> Success in the art of fieldwork depends, to a considerable extent, on establishing a very special role that legitimatizes a kind of information-getting behavior that was not previously part of

social expectations within the community. They may identify
with local inhabitants . . . but the role of gatherer of information, persistent questioner and stranger from another culture is
always part of one's social identity. (1978, p. 182)

Throughout the study I strived to achieve this role, for as a member of
the community, a mother of two children who learned to read (in the
traditional sense) during the course of research, and a visitor to the
United States, I attempted to be both friend and inquisitor, insider
and outsider in a foreign land.

At the conclusion of the study I visited each family to discuss the
monograph I had written and to ask them how they regarded my
relationship with them. Their responses were enlightening, and in
retrospect it is very clear that my relationship with each family was
highly dependent upon the unique interaction of our biographical and
personal idiosyncracies. Barry Lindell, who is intensely involved in
his own research endeavors, said he regarded me as an "inquisitor and
not a propagator." Laura Lindell said I was a good friend who was a
serious researcher, and then added that she was not fooled by the
whimsical way in which I talked about my research. Karen Farley
also said I was easy to talk to and added that she did not think of me as
a researcher. Lee Farley commented that he was aware that I was
British, and smiling he explained, "You deal a little more formally
with the British." Leo Langdon recounted to me that when I had first
come to their home, he had said to Jill, his wife, "What do we know
about her? Where does she live? She comes here and talks to our ·
children and we know nothing about her!" Jill laughed remembering the conversation, and she said that had been a long time ago,
adding that she had enjoyed helping. I asked Jill if my presence had
been intrusive, and she replied, "No. It was never a problem." Dan
Dawson described me as a friend with a project, and Jessie Dawson
explained that she had enjoyed taking part in the research as it made
her think of things she needed to clarify in her own mind. Azar Simms
laughed when I asked him, and with a twinkle in his eye said, "You're
just the sweetest girl." Nina's response was more complicated. She
said I was "almost a friend," and then she explained that she did not
know what category to put me into. She said there was "always an
element of business in our meetings," and she was not sure "where
research ends and friendship begins." Nina concluded by saying she
hoped I would visit them when the project was over, but that she was
not sure I would. When I visited the Kings, Joe left Donna to answer
my question. Donna thought for a while and then said, "You like to

talk, and you like to tell stories and to listen to stories." She explained that speaking as a psychologist, I was not her image of a researcher since I was not organized with a series of questions. Donna said she felt I probably "elicited stuff" that many researchers would miss because when she talked to me she did not feel she had to stick to any specific topic. Then she added, "You never know what's business and what's not business." Donna went on to say that I was "considerate to a fault and too worried about intruding," and she concluded rather paradoxically by saying I brought an informality to the situation that made it easy for her to talk with me.

The parents' comments point to a number of things that affected the relationships we built over the three years of the study. First of all, the relationships were greatly affected by their expectations of me as a friend and as a researcher. For the Lindells, Dawsons, and Farleys, I was primarily a friend; I knew each of these families prior to their participation in the study. For the Simmses, Langdons, and Kings, my initial introduction was as a researcher. The Langdons and Kings did not speak of friendship in our discussions of their images of me, and although Donna King stated that I was not her image of a researcher, she responded to my question in terms of my research.

The precarious nature of the researcher's role is perhaps most visible in Nina Simms's comment that she was not sure where research ended and friendship began. During one of my visits we sat gossiping, and after she had regaled me with yet another tale, she banged her hands on the table and said, "What else? Don't you have a list of things? You know. Get yourself a list you can ask everybody," to which I replied, "I have a list." In retropsect, my reply only added to the ambiguity of the situation, for although I reassured family members when they questioned the relevance of the tales they told, I never gave an in-depth explanation of participant-observer research methods. My comments that everything was relevant since I was studying literacy in family life were insufficient to alter their conceptions of research. The psychologist's experimental methods seemed uppermost in their minds. However, although on one level this might be viewed as an indictment of the way I presented myself to the families, from another perspective it enabled me to share stories which were not specifically constructed to reveal literate events. Thus, when Nina Simms told me of her proclivity for getting lost as a small child, she did not relate it to reading, and I had no idea whether the story was relevant or not. A year later, after I listened to an audiorecording of her reading to Andrew about a little boy and an elephant who got lost, and talking to him about his getting lost in a shopping mall, I reminded Nina of her earlier story. She again recounted her memories of her parents' distress when she had "gone for walks" alone as a very small child. Nina then spoke of her father's response when she told him of Andrew getting lost. Her father laughed and said, "Nina, you were the worst." This historical perspective provided me with an example of temporal integration that otherwise would have been lost. Clearly, sharing stories without being inhibited about whether they are relevant to young children learning to read and write has its advantages.

Involving the Families in the Research Process

Throughout the study, every effort was made to protect the families' right to privacy. One of the major considerations was how to gain access to their lives without becoming too intrusive (Taylor, 1981). How much of family life can a researcher reasonably ask a family to share? Where are the boundaries and how are they to be established? These issues were raised indirectly by each of the families during the initial phases of the study and recurred many times as the research progressed.

During the early conversations several parents spoke of sharing stories with their children at bedtime. Clearly such occasions were of importance to the study, and yet the parents and I considered observation at such times too disruptive as well as intrusive. The dilemma was openly discussed with the families. Four of the families agreed to audiorecord the stories, while two of the families felt it would be too disruptive. However, they agreed to record stories that were read earlier in the day. Interestingly, many months later, both of these families presented me with further tapes—of bedtime stories.

Gaining access without intrusion was a daily concern, especially in a study that lasted for three years. Being raised on an overpopulated island of inveterate gossips has its advantages, for I learned as a child how to fashion my intense interest in people to fit within the boundaries of what is acceptable. This part of my heritage resulted in the research style which shaped the negotiations of access. The schedules of the families are fast moving, and as they have stated, time is their biggest problem. Most of the fathers work extraordinarily long hours; thus my primary contact with each of the families was with the mother, and my visits with the fathers were carefully negotiated.

The arrangements were different with each family. The Lindells lived a considerable distance from my home, and so when I visited them I often stayed to dinner and sometimes overnight. The Lindells also visited my home, and the children sometimes stayed with me. The Dawsons' hectic schedules left little time for casual visits. In the first year of the study, Jessie was working part time as a legal secretary and as an aide in the library at Ellie's school. In the following years, she worked on a full-time basis in the library. After school she ferried her children to their various ballet classes. There was very little time for my visits, but fortunately the carefully planned times we arranged were more than supplemented by the many casual conversations Jessie and I had when she stopped to talk to me as I watched my children playing in the street. In addition, both Sissie and Hannah babysat for me, and Ellie occasionally played with Louise.

The Farley schedule was a little different. Nan was still a baby, and Karen spent most of her days caring for her. There was no need for elaborate arrangements, and I often popped in to visit them. I always avoided going between 12:30 and 3:00 as that was when Nan and Debbie slept. Karen used to say she would "kill" if anyone called and woke them up. In addition, Kathy and Debbie often played with Louise and Ben, so I had opportunities to observe them while they played.

The Simms family lived in a nearby town, and so my visits were planned, sometimes a few days in advance and other times heralded by a quick phone call. Nina Simms told Azar that she was taking part in the research, and she said that although he did not mind her participating, he did not want to himself. For almost a year he did not take part. Then Nina arranged for me to visit them on a Saturday afternoon when she knew he would be home. Azar did not ask me any specific questions regarding the research. We talked of Margaret Thatcher and the British elections and about life in the United States. After this brief introduction, Azar agreed to participate in the study.

The Langdon family live close to Nina and Azar Simms, so my visits were usually prearranged. I often visited them in the afternoons, arriving some time before Ken came home from school and staying until dinner time.

The King family lived a little nearer to my home, but their busy work schedules dictated my visits. I often saw Donna in the mornings, and special arrangements were made for me to visit the family when Bonnie came home from school, for Donna worked several afternoons and the other afternoons were usually tied up with the children's classes (gymnastics, tumbling, art).

In addition to these many meetings, serendipity was in my favor. I have been to parties at the Lindells, and the Dawsons had a Christmas party to which the Farleys as well as myself and David, my husband, were invited. Jessie and I have been on book hunts in New York City when she was looking for new books for her library, and Dan has been to dinner at my home when Jessie and the girls were away in Maine. Karen Farley has often invited Louise, Ben, and me to go swimming, and we have visited nearby parks in the spring and apple farms in the fall. Nina Simms has invited me to her Tupperware parties, and she and her family have visited my home. Jill Langdon has also visited my home, bringing her children to play with Louise and Ben; Donna King has often brought James around for morning coffee. In addition, I have been fortunate enough to meet many relatives of the families, and I have recorded conversations with the mothers of Karen Farley and Donna King. Although my visits were negotiated to fit busy schedules, there were often occasions for more casual meetings.

Schneider states, "The fundamental rule of fieldwork is that the informant is seldom if ever wrong, never provides irrelevant data, and is incapable of pure fabrication" (1968, p. 11). The research proceeded from this perspective, for as Leichter so aptly states, "Even gossip and critical stories about the experiences of family members and others can provide opportunities for formulating and clarifying ideas" (1978, p. 210). Thus, all stories were relevant, and I tried to reassure the families that the information they gave me was important, even the funny things which seemed of little consequence. Perhaps what impressed them more than my reassurances were the stories that I told. I shared with them tales of my childhood and of my children. I talked of my ambivalence as to staying in the United States, and I spoke of some of my worst moments as a mother. It was perhaps my willingness to be as revealing as I expected the families to be that made our conversations so easy. Nina once commented that it helped that I also had bad days of motherhood.

I often talked with a family about the tales the other families told me. Then I listened as they juxtaposed this tale with their own familial situation and constructed further interpretations of the data. This was an interactive process, a reciprocal agreement of back and forth in which verification changed in complexity as it became part of the process of discovery (Diesing, 1971). Thus, when Laura Lindell spoke of her children's intense interest in word games during their kindergarten years, I talked of this with the parents in the other families. Such a shift toward more specific activities was noted by all of the families, and they told tales about their children's kindergarten and first-grade years. A year later, my observations of Debbie, Andrew, and Steven as they prepared for their kindergarten year added another dimension to the interpretations I had constructed with the parents. Speaking of the anthropologist, Varenne writes, "Like the *bricoleur*, the scientist starts with odds and ends, pieces of events, singular occurrences" (1977, p. 224). This is an apt description of the way Laura Lindell's comments eventually led to the interpretations presented in the fourth chapter!

The Reactions of the Families to the Manuscript

Perhaps of greatest importance in weighing old perspectives and building new ones are the views of the families who gave of their time to this study. The families' comments add another dimension to the study.

When the manuscript was nearing completion I asked each family to read what I had written. Rather than encumber them with some 300 pages of burgeoning text, I selected several chapters for them to read. I gave each family copies of (1) the original introduction containing a detailed outline of each chapter, (2) the revised introduction focusing more upon the findings of the study, and (3) chapter 4 providing representative examples of the ways I had presented the field research data.

I talked with each mother, saying I was interested in her reaction to what I had written. When asked to be more specific I explained that I was particularly interested in knowing how she felt about the way I had represented her family and what she thought of the perspectives of family literacy I was developing. To prepare them for the experience of seeing themselves in print I used the analogy of listening to a tape recording of one's voice for the first time.

In the following weeks the mothers and several of the older children shared with me their reactions to the chapters. Most of their initial comments focused upon how easy it was to read the document. One mother commented that she had sat with the dictionary beside her and that she had been relieved when she did not have to use it. Many of the mothers talked of flipping through the pages to find their families. Laura Lindell noted that it was "the personal things that had appealed" to her, while Karen Farley commented on how funny it was to see the things they had said in print. These initial comments led to discussions on the characterization of the families. Jill Langdon said that the writings had "caught the flavor" of her family, and she and her husband had been pleased that I had been able to achieve such an accurate portrayal of them. Several of the mothers spoke of particular members of their families whom they felt were especially well represented. Interestingly, one of the older children, Beth Lindell, commented that she could see her family in what she read and that even the names seemed right. She explained that when she began reading she thought of the girl in the text as herself but as she read a subtle change took place and she became the girl in the text. She said now strange it was and then concluded by saying "even the name could be mine."

I was pleased the families could see themselves in what I had written, for in writing I had tried to lift them from the pages so the reader could touch their lives. This was essential if the reader was to gain an appreciation for the many ways literacy is a part of the families' social world. However, such visualizations can be viewed from another perspective. This was emphasized by Donna King who spoke of her "feelings of being exposed" by the document, and she commented on several examples in the text which she was finding it difficult to share. She said, "I don't know if I want to share them with other people because they are so precious to me." I explained the importance of the examples to the perspectives of family literacy I was developing and together we made several changes in the text. Based upon my explanations Donna seemed to be more comfortable with the inclusion of the examples; however, she emphasized that she felt I was assuming too much of the reader and that more specific explanations should be given in the text of why each example was included.

In response to the issues Donna raised, I talked again with the other mothers. Their reactions reconfirmed the positions they had presented on first reading the chapters. Karen Farley emphasized that seeing her family in print had not been a problem. She explained she could "see her own kids" in the experiences of the other families and in some way this verified her own family's experiences. She also stated that she would be comfortable with her friends reading the document. Jessie Dawson responded to my question by stating that everything I wrote "was extremely accurate," and then she emphasized that if she had felt misrepresented she would have been extremely upset. She stressed that one of the reasons she and her husband had been so pleased with the document was because I had presented the examples without interjecting myself into them.

Although most of the families had no reservations about the document, one family felt differently. No research project is important enough to cause anxious moments for any of the participants. The onus is on the researcher to alleviate the anxiety in any way she can. In this particular instance I worked with Donna King in changing some of the sentences, phrases, and words that she found unacceptable. As she was also worried that her family was identifiable in the text, I changed the details about her family not directly relevant to the study. The one comment I did not act upon was her feeling that specific explanations were needed as to why each example was included; the imagery in the examples is so strong that any words I might add would only detract from the pictures it creates.

WRITING

Mead writes, "Everything that happens . . .. becomes data once the event has been noted, written up, photographed or tape recorded" (1977, p. 6). Torn scraps of paper and verbatim transcriptions as well as analytic memos and working notes are among the multiple levels of data on which this study is based, for while the scraps of paper provide insights into the writings of the children, the working notes provide insights into the development of my perspectives. In retrospect, it is only through the presentation of such multiple levels of data that the intuitive and analytic processes in the research endeavor can be made visible (Taylor, 1978b). Thus, this section reflects the movement toward a fuller understanding of the multiple interpretations of family literacy that evolved as the study progressed.

Chapter 2, which focused on family literacy and conservation and change in the transmission of literacy styles and values, began when the study began. Armed with a list of questions based on the questionnaire developed by Durkin (1966) in her seminal study of early readers, I visited the Lindell family. However, following the questions was not easy, for both Laura and Barry had their own agendas. They moved easily between the past and the present as they wove together events which would have seemed disconnected had the question-answer format been strictly observed. The more formal discussions quickly gave way to conversation, and questions relating to literacy were dispersed into the more general exchange of ideas.

These early conversations were audiorecorded and transcribed. From these transcripts I constructed my initial interpretations, later tested as I moved between the families sharing stories and ideas, adding their comments to the data. As the discussions proceeded, I also sought support for the ideas which were emerging by reading the literature relevant to the idea of multigenerational patterns. The concepts of conservation and change originated in the Lowell Lectures of Albert North Whitehead (1925), and the writings of Dewey

(1922) supported my perspectives. As the themes of conservation and change emerged, I began to transfer many of the parents' comments to a series of index cards. These cards also contained my notes (sometimes referred to as analytic memos) and references to texts relevant to the emerging themes. My working notes were written from the transcripts and index cards. Finally, using every level of data, I constructed the monograph.

In writing the chapter on multigenerational patterns in the transmission of literacy styles and values, it became increasingly evident that another equally relevant perspective of family literacy deserved attention. While family members mediated their children's experiences of learning to read and write, they also used reading and writing to mediate their experiences of one another. Literacy could be viewed as contributing to the social organization of the everyday lives of the families. Thus, the existing audiorecordings and transcripts were viewed from a different perspective, and many of the families' comments were transferred to a second series of index cards. However, new methods of data collection were needed to tap the information that I was seeking.

It seemed important to gain detailed lists of the reading and writing materials in each home. However, to go through the families' homes with a notebook and pencil would have been too intrusive (as well as tedious!). This dilemma was solved by Nina Simms. One morning, I told her of my interest in the reading and writing materials in the families' homes. Nina suggested that I look around, and together we conducted a search. A small audiorecorder with a wriststrap enabled me to take part in the explorations without having to resort to cumbersome and intrusive note taking. As we progressed from room to room, Nina took books, which had been hers as a child, from the bookshelves and pulled dusty boxes of educational games from obscure corners. In the bedrooms, Andrew joined in by piling books on his bedroom floor, sharing his favorite stories, and pointing out those books which had been written in or torn. In a very real sense, both mother and son assumed the role of anthropologist (Schneider, 1968, p. 12), and the extraordinarily rich data that resulted far exceeded the usefulness of any simple listing of the materials in Nina's home. Nina's approach to data collection provided me with an excellent way of collecting some of the data I needed if the perspective of literacy and the social organization of everyday life was to be achieved, and I used this approach with the parents and children in each family.

Although the data I was collecting was insightful, much of the families' writing made its way into the garbage, and I needed to intercept this flow. Thus, during my visits I looked for the odd scraps of paper which were usually lying round and asked if I could look at them. At one of Nina Simms's Tupperware parties I watched Carol participate in the pencil-and-paper games organized by the Tupperware representative. When the demonstrations and games were completed, the participants were invited to view the products. It was at that point that Nina found me searching under the cushions on her couch for the paper on which Carol (who had since gone to bed) had written. Nina laughed in disbelief. What did I want with such a scrap of paper? Nina's reaction was typical of the families' response for my kleptomaniacal interest in their writings.

To further supplement the data I was collecting in this haphazard way, I asked each family to collect everything the children wrote for one week. Then, using the approach that I developed when the families recorded stories for me, I visited each family and sat with the mothers while they showed me the papers they had accumulated. I learned much of what the children wrote, and I also learned much of their mothers' perceptions of these endeavors. This information together with notes of my observations of the children and framed by the literature search formed the basis of my interpretations of family literacy presented in chapter 3.

In developing this perspective, I wrote of the children actively constructing the functions of written language as they used print in their everyday lives, but I had written little of the ways that the children came to learn of the form of written language. The perspective of chapter 4 filled this gap. I continued to visit the families and collect data, sharing my interpretations of literacy, but no new data collection procedures were employed. Instead, I reviewed the data I had collected, considering it from the perspective of another literature, in an attempt to discover some insights into the ways the children learned of the symbols, signs, and texts which filled their world. The information was already there, hidden in the multiple levels of data.

Chapters 5 and 6 were written to view from a broader perspective the interpretations of family literacy I had developed. In chapter 5 I emphasized the families' belief that just as their children had learned to talk, they would learn to read and write. Their belief was implicit in the data I had collected, and I had considered this idea since the first year of the study. However, at the conclusion of the study I asked the families, "What if one of the children failed?" At this time, and with considerable trepidation, I decided to include data on several adults and one eleven-year-old boy who had, in the eyes of society, failed. I did not include Myra's and Ernie's comments for the purpose of some simple counterpoint, for we are too quick to compare people whose lives bear no comparison. In juxtaposing their experiences I hoped to raise questions about the multiple meanings of literacy in the lives of those whom we seek to study and teach. The implications of this viewpoint are presented in chapter 6. In writing, I have attempted to raise the questions of whether we can seriously expect children who have never experienced, or have limited experience of, reading and writing as complex cultural activities to successfully learn to read and write from the narrowly defined pedagogical practices of our schools. Within this context I have called for research focusing on the ways children, growing up in a variety of social settings, initiate, absorb, and synthesize the educational influences in their environment and for public and cooperative literacy programs purposefully designed to introduce prekindergarten and kindergarten children to the uses of print.

An essential (often forgotten) element of reconstruction in ethnographic research is the requirement that the information be presented in a way that those reading the account can decide for themselves whether or not they accept the interpretations of the researcher (McDermott, Gospodinoff, and Aron, 1978). Moving through the multiple levels of field research, I have attempted to share some of the theoretical perspectives, issues, and concerns that shaped the study, so readers can judge for themselves the validity of the family literacy perspectives I have developed. No single reconstruction exhausts all possible interpretations, and it is hoped that there is sufficient information for alternative explanations to be considered.

References

Anderson, A.B., W.B. Teale, and E. Estrada. 1980. Low income children's preschool literacy experiences: Some naturalistic observations. *The Quarterly Newsletter of the Laboratory for Human Cognition* 2−3:59−65.

Anderson, N. 1977. A question of meaning. *Cambridge Journal of Education* 7:105−113.

Aries, P. 1962. *Centuries of childhood: A social history of family life*, trans R. Baldick. New York: Vintage Books.

Au, K.H.P. 1980. Participation structures in a reading lesson with Hawaiian children: Analysis of a culturally appropriate instructional event. Manuscript, Kamehameha Early Education Program, Honolulu, Hawaii.

Bamberger, R. 1974. Literature and development in reading. In *New horizons in reading*, ed. J. Merritt. Newark, Del.: International Reading Association.

Bar-Tal, D. 1978. Attributional analysis of achievement-related behavior. *Review of Educational Research* 48:259−271.

Bateson, M.C. 1980. Continuities in insight and innovation: Toward a biography of Margaret Mead. *American Anthropologist* 82:270−277.

Beattie, J. 1964. *Other cultures*. New York: The Free Press.

Berreman, G.D. 1972. Is ethnoscience relevant? In *Culture and cognition: Rules, maps, and plans*, ed. J.P. Spradley. New York: Chandler.

Birdwhistell, R.L. 1977. Some discussion of ethnography, theory and method. In *About Bateson: Essays on Gregory Bateson*, ed. J. Brockman. New York: E.P. Dutton.

Bissex, G.L. 1980. *GNYS AT WRK: A child learns to write and read*. Cambridge: Harvard University Press.

Britton, James. 1970. Language and Learning. London: Penguin

Bond, G.L., and R. Dykstra. 1967. The cooperative research program in first-grade reading instruction. *Reading Research Quarterly* 2(4):5−126.

Bullock Report. 1975. *A Language for Life*. London: HMSO.

Cazden, C. 1980. Keynote address presented at The Language of Young Children: Frontiers of Research, Brooklyn College, New York.

Chomsky, C. 1969. *The acquisition of syntax in children from five to ten*. Cambridge: MIT Press.

Chukovsky, K. 1968. *From two to five*. Berkeley: University of California Press.

Clay, M.M. 1972. *Reading: The patterning of complex behavior*. London: Heinemann.

Cohen, D.H. 1968. The effect of literature on vocabulary and reading achievement. *Elementary English* 45:209–213.

Cremin, L.A. 1970. *American education: The colonial experience 1607–1783*. New York: Harper Torchbooks.

Dewey, J. 1922. *Human nature and conduct*. New York: Random House, rpt. 1957.

Diesing, P. 1971. *Patterns of discovery in the social sciences*. Chicago: Aldine.

Durkin, D. 1966. *Children who read early*. New York: Teachers College Press.

Ehri, L.C. 1978. Beginning reading from a psycholinguistic perspective: Amalgamation of word identities. In *The recognition of words*, eds. L.C. Ehri, R.W. Barron, and J.M. Feldman. Newark, Del.: International Reading Association.

Farnsworth, K. 1978. Personal communication, Englewood Library, Englewood, N.J.

Farr, R., and S. Weintraub. 1974–1975. Methodological incarceration. *Reading Research Quarterly* 10(4).

Ferreiro, E. 1978. What is written in a written sentence? A developmental answer. *Journal of Education* 160(4):25–39.

Forester, A.D. 1975. Learning the language of reading. *Alberta Journal of Educational Research* 21:56–62.

Forester, A.D., and N.I. Mickelson. 1979. Language acquisition and learning to read. In *Applied linguistics and reading*, ed. R.E. Shafer. Newark, Del.: International Reading Association.

Gans, H.J. 1962. *Urban villagers*. New York: The Free Press.

Geertz, C. 1973. *The interpretation of cultures*. New York: Basic Books.

Glaser, B.G., and A.L. Strauss. 1973. *The discovery of grounded theory: Strategies for qualitative research*. Chicago: Aldine.

Goffman, E. 1971. *Relations in public*. New York: Harper Colophon Books.

Goodman, K.S., Y.M. Goodman, and C. Burke. 1978. Reading for life: The psycholinguistic base. In *Reading: Implementing the Bullock Report*, eds. E. Hunter-Grundin and H.V. Grundin. London: Ward Lock Educational.

Goody, J. 1968. *Literacy in traditional societies*. Cambridge: Cambridge University Press.

Gough, P.B. 1972. One second of reading. In *Language by ear and eye*, eds. J.F. Kavanagh and I.G. Mattingly. Cambridge: MIT Press.

Hale, A. 1980. The social relationships implicit in approaches to reading. *Reading* 14(2):24—30.

Halliday, M.A.K. 1973. *Explorations in the functions of language*. London: Edward Arnold.

Harste, J.C., C.L. Burke, and V.A. Woodward. 1981. *Children, their language and world: Initial encounters with print*. National Institute of Education (NIE-G-79-0132).

Hegel, G.W.F. 1967. *The phenomenology of the mind*, trans. J.W. Ballie. New York: Harper Torchbooks.

Hildreth, G. 1936. Developmental sequences in name writing. *Child Development* 7:291—301.

Hill, C., and H. Varenne. 1979. Family language and education: The sociolinguistic model of restricted and elaborated codes. Manuscript, Columbia University Teachers College.

Hill, J. 1974. *Children are people: The librarian in the community*. New York: Crowell.

Holdaway, D. 1979. *The foundations of literacy*. Sydney: Ashton Scholastic.

Huey, E.B. 1908. *The psychology and pedagogy of reading*. Cambridge: MIT Press, rpt. 1973.

Hunter, D., and D. Harman. 1979. *Adult illiteracy in the United States*. New York: McGraw-Hill.

Hunter-Grundin, E. 1979. *Literacy: A systematic start*. New York: Harper & Row.

Hymes, D. 1974. *Foundations in sociolinguistics: An ethnographic approach*. Philadelphia: University of Pennsylvania Press.

Istomina, Z.M. 1948. The development of voluntary memory in pre-school-age children. *Soviet Psychology* 13:5—64, rpt. 1974—1975.

Kaplan, A. 1964. *The conduct of inquiry: Methodology for behavioral science*. New York: Chandler.

Kavale, K.A. 1977. Adult basic education: Has it worked? *Journal of Reading* 20:368—375.

LaBerge, D., and S. Samuels. 1974. Toward a theory of automatic information processing in reading. *Cognitive Psychology* 6:293—323.

Labov, W. 1979. Competing value systems in the inner-city schools. In *Ethnography and education: Children in and out of school*, ed. P. Gilmore. Philadelphia: University of Pennsylvania Press.

Langer, S.K. 1960. *Philosophy in a new key*. Cambridge: Harvard University Press.

Leichter, H.J. 1973. The concept of educative style. *Teachers College Record* 75:239—250.

Leichter, H.J. 1974. The family as educator. *Teachers College Record* 76: 175–217. Rpt. in *The family as educator*, ed. H.J. Leichter. New York: Teachers College Press, 1977.

Leichter, H.J. 1978. Families and communities as educators: Some concepts of relationship. *Teachers College Records* 79:567–658.

Leichter, H.J., and W.E. Mitchell. 1978. *Kinship and casework: Family networks and social intervention.* New York: Teachers College Press.

Magoon, A.J. 1977. Constructivist approaches in educational research. *Review of Educational Research* 47:651–693.

McDermott, R.P. 1976. Achieving school failure: An anthropological approach to illiteracy and social stratification. In *Theoretical models and processes of reading*, 2nd ed., eds. H. Singer and R. Rudell. Newark, Del.: International Reading Association.

McDermott, R.P. 1977. The ethnography of speaking and reading. In *Linguistic theory: What can it say about reading?* ed. R.W. Shuy. Newark, Del.: International Reading Association.

McDermott, R.P. 1978. Some reasons for focusing on classrooms in reading research. In *The twenty-seventh yearbook of the National Reading Conference.* Milwaukee, Wisc.: National Reading Conference.

McDermott, R.P., K. Gospodinoff, and J. Aron. 1978. Criteria for an ethnographically adequate description of concerted activities and their contexts. *Semiotica* 24:245–275.

Mead, M. 1943. Our educational emphases in primitive perspectives. *American Journal of Sociology* 48:633–639.

Mead, M. 1956. *New lives for old: Cultural transformation—Manus. 1928–1953.* New York: William Morrow.

Mead, M. 1977. *Letters from the field, 1925–1975.* New York: Harper & Row.

Mead, M. 1978. The evocation of psychologically relevant responses in ethnological fieldwork. In *The making of psychological anthropology*, ed. G.D. Spindler. Berkeley: University of California Press.

Mead, M., and R. Metraux. 1953. *The study of culture at a distance.* Chicago: University of Chicago Press.

Medawar, P.B. 1979. Advice to a young scientist. *Harper's* 259:39–46.

Merleau-Ponty, M. 1973. *The prose of the world.* Northwestern University Studies in Phenomenology and Existential Philosophy. Evanston, Ill.: Northwestern University Press.

Mishler, E.G. 1979. Meaning in context: Is there any other kind? *Harvard Educational Review* 49:1–19.

Neisser, U. 1979. *Memory: What are the important questions?* In *Practical applications of memory*, eds. M.M. Gruneburg, P.M. Morris, and R.N. Sykes. London: Academic Press.

Paley, V.G. 1981. *Walley's stories.* Cambridge: Harvard University Press.

Pelto, P.J., and G.H. Pelto. 1978. *Anthropological research: The structure of inquiry.* New York: Cambridge University Press.

Radcliffe-Brown, A.R. 1965. *Structure and function in primitive society.* New York: The Free Press.

Read, C. 1975. The preschool orthographer. In *Foundations of language development*, eds. E. Lennenberg and E. Lennenberg. New York: Academic Press.

Riesman, D. 1955. The oral tradition, the written word, and the screen image. Keynote address presented at the dedication of the Olive Kettering Library, Antioch College Founders Day.

Rist, R.C. 1980. Blitzkrieg ethnography: On the transformation of a method into a movement. *Educational Researcher* 9(2):8–10.

Samuels, S.J. 1971. Letter-name versus letter-sound knowledge in learning to read. *The Reading Teacher* 24:604–608.

Sartre, J.P. 1964. *The words*, trans. B. Frechtman. New York: George Braziller.

Schneider, D.M. 1968. *American kinship: A cultural account.* Englewood Cliffs, N.J.: Prentice-Hall.

Scribner, S. 1980. Comments made at the Ethnography in Education Research Forum, University of Pennsylvania.

Scribner, S., and M. Cole. 1978a. Unpackaging literacy. *Social Science Information* 17:19–40.

Scribner, S., and M. Cole. 1978b. Literacy without schooling: Testing for intellectual effects. *Harvard Educational Review* 48:448–461.

Scribner, S., and M. Cole. 1981. *The psychology of literacy.* Cambridge: Harvard University Press.

Shuttles, G.D. 1968. *The social order of the slum.* Chicago: University of Chicago Press.

Southgate, V. 1972. Literacy at all levels. In *Literacy at all levels*, ed. V. Southgate. London: Ward Lock Educational.

Spradley, J.P. 1979. *The ethnographic interview.* New York: Holt, Rinehart & Winston.

Strickland, D.S. 1971. The effects of a special literature program on the oral language of linguistically different Negro kindergarten children. Unpublished doctoral dissertation, New York University.

Sulzby, E. 1981. *Kindergarteners begin to read their own compositions: Beginning readers' developing knowledges about written language project.* Final Report to the Research Foundation of the National Council of Teachers of English.

Sutton-Smith, B., and B.G. Rosenberg. 1970. *The sibling*. New York: Holt, Rinehart & Winston.

Szwed, J.F. 1977. The ethnography of literacy. Paper presented at the National Institute of Education Conference on Writing, Los Angeles.

Taylor, D. 1978a. The role of intuition in the acquisition of knowledge. Manuscript, Columbia University Teachers College.

Taylor, D. 1978b. The social consequences of illiteracy. Manuscript, Columbia University Teachers College.

Taylor, D. 1980. Learning to "read" stories. Paper presented at the Ethnography in Education Research Forum, University of Pennsylvania.

Taylor, D. 1981. The family and the development of reading skills and values. *The Journal of Research in Reading* 4(2):92–103.

Taylor, D. 1982. Translating children's everyday uses of print into classroom practice. *Language Arts* 59(6):546–549.

Taylor, D. In press. Children's Social Use of Print. *The Reading Teacher*.

Tolstoy, L. 1967. *Tolstoy on education*, trans. L. Wiener. Chicago: University of Chicago Press.

Varenne, H. 1977. *Americans together: Structured diversity in a midwestern town*. New York: Teachers College Press.

Vygotsky, L.S. 1962. *Thought and language*, trans. E. Hanfmann and G. Vakar. Cambridge: MIT Press.

Vygotsky, L.S. 1978. *Mind in society: The development of higher psychological processes*. Cambridge: Harvard University Press.

Whitehead, A.N. 1925. Requisites for social progress. In *Science and the modern world*. New York: The Free Press, rpt. 1967.

Wolf, R., and B.L. Tymitz. 1976–1977. Ethnography and reading: Matching inquiry mode to process. *Reading Research Quarterly* 12(1).